ADVANCE

PHYLICIA FANT
Global Head of Music, Amazon

"Sheard is a marketing savant who channels his expertise by exploring the mutually beneficial relationship brands must embrace to ensure their legacies. His passion for this union is a call to action for global unity to protect our one shared gift."

MARCELLO BOTTOLI
Founder, EVCP Growth Equity; Former CEO, Louis Vuitton

"Bob Sheard has written a uniquely dream-fuelling book. He is a one-of-a-kind visionary who sees through what creates unique brands with perennial legacies. This is necessary food for thought for whoever has an interest in meaningful brands."

ROGER WADE
Chairman, BoxFund

"I've always been deeply passionate about product and branding. Throughout my 35-year career in consumer brands, I've rarely sought advice on branding from third-party consultants. However, Bob Sheard and his team at FreshBritain are a remarkable exception. When Bob speaks about branding, you listen. His expertise is unmatched. It's been an honour to work with him and his team, and I'm proud to collaborate with such a leader in the field."

SIMON MOTTRAM
Founder, Rapha Performance Roadwear

"Brands and branding are concepts that everyone seems to know about today, but the difference between brands as veneer and brands we can believe in has never been more stark or more important. Bob's book gives valuable guidance on how to build brands that will succeed and last."

NICLAS BORNLING
Brand Director, Salomon Group
"More than anything else, Bob forced truth and focus through the collaborative process involving many strong opinions from a diverse array of cultural backgrounds. This search for truth can and should be a testing journey, but it will always strip away that which doesn't matter and inevitably unveil the true beauty about a brand. Salomon has and will always be Mountain Sports Innovation for Mountain Sports Athletes. What Bob showed me during those days in Chamonix has guided me ever since in my professional career. I'm forever grateful for those lessons. Thank you, Bob."

BEAR GRYLLS
Adventurer
"Well Done!"

OLYA KURYSHCHUK
Founder, One Granary Square
"Bob Sheard's vision of regenerative branding isn't just an idea—it's a movement waiting to take shape. This book is a game-changer for business leaders who want to create brands that don't just sell but truly make a difference in the world."

LADY CAROLE BAMFORD
Founder, Daylesford Organic
"In a world where planet and people must come above profit, this book is essential. A refreshing and innovative approach to building a business while shaping a more sustainable future"

ANNABEL THOMAS
Founder, Nc'nean
"Bob is a visionary. The one who can sort the wheat from the chaff, with an uncanny ability to articulate clear visions, cohesive statements and holistic viewpoints, which everyone else wishes they could have seen first. Branding is all about storytelling, and stories need to be simple for people to remember them. Bob's ability to create these simples stories is the core of his brilliance."

HERVÉ BERTRAND
Senior Vice President & Design Director, Geely Commercial Vehicles
"What brands need is a clear customer experience, a sound motto. Bob manages to define an articulate brand narrative to establish brand direction and stability. FreshBritain has been at the forefront of brand building, and in this troubled time where nothing makes sense anymore, Bob and his team manage to create a clear sense and order with proven and remarkable acumen."

TAHA BAWA
Co-Founder, Goodwall
"Sheard delivers a bold guide to the future of branding. He challenges brands to move beyond storytelling and truly stand out. An inspiring must-read for leaders in an increasing competitive landscape."

REBECCA WRIGHT (SHE/HER/HERS)
Dean of S School, Central Saint Martins
"Bob is a restless disruptor whose book envisions a potentially radical re-imagining of how the relationship between brands, business and education could re-shape our world."

Published by
LID Publishing
An imprint of LID Business Media Ltd.
LABS House, 15–19 Bloomsbury Way,
London, WC1A 2TH, UK

info@lidpublishing.com
www.lidpublishing.com

A member of:
BPR
businesspublishersroundtable.com

All rights reserved. Without limiting the rights under copyright reserved, no part of this publication may be reproduced, stored or introduced into a retrieval system, or transmitted, in any form or by any means (electronic, mechanical, photocopying, recording or otherwise) without the prior written permission of both the copyright owners and the publisher of this book.

© Bob Sheard, 2025
© LID Business Media Limited, 2025

Printed by Gutenberg Press, Malta
ISBN: 978-1-917391-28-3
ISBN: 978-1-917391-29-0 (ebook)

THE BRAND NEW FUTURE

How brands can save the world.

by Bob Sheard

MADRID | MEXICO CITY | LONDON
BUENOS AIRES | BOGOTA | SHANGHAI

CONTENTS

1. HOW BRANDS WORK
1.1 Why Brands?   25
1.2 Why Now?   28
1.3 Prosperity and Population   42
1.4 Brand Strategy   44
1.5 Humans as Storytellers   46

2. CONVENTIONAL BRAND DESIGN
2.1 Brand Design: Delivering Growth   50
2.2 Brand Design: Delivering Revenue   50
2.3 Brand Design: Delivering Profit   68

3. BRAND ROLES
3.1 Rebel   103
3.2 Leader   105
3.3 Child   107
3.4 Guide   108
3.5 Purist   110
3.6 Adventurer   111
3.7 Trickster   113
3.8 Craftsman   114
3.9 Warrior   116
3.10 Guardian   118
3.11 Partner   119
3.12 Lover   120
3.13 Visionary   120

3.14	Tribe	122
3.15	Everyman	123
3.16	Anti-Hero	124

4. BRAND PRACTICE

4.1	Brand Practice — Storytelling	130
4.2	Brand Practice — Product Design	131
4.3	Brand Practice — Communication Design	140
4.4	Brand Practice — Product Architecture	150
4.5	Brand Practice — Diffusion of Influence	156
4.6	Brand Practice — Activation	158

5. THE FUTURE OF EVERYTHNG

5.1	A History of Brand Communication	168
5.2	A New Form of Growth (Generations Driving Change)	169
5.3	But Why Gen Z?	171
5.4	Corporate Protocols	172
5.5	Brand Protocols	172
5.6	Product Protocols	173
5.7	The Three Big Cs: COVID-19, Climate and Conflict	173
5.8	Making More with Less	175

6. GROWTH IN PERPETUITY (IN THEORY)

6.1	Brands — A Living System Perspective	187
6.2	Regenerative Brand Thinking	189
6.3	Regenerative Corporate Protocols	190
6.4	Regenerative Brand Protocols	192
6.5	Regenerative Product Protocols	195

7. GROWTH IN PERPETUITY (IN PRACTICE)

7.1	Reimagine Beliefs as Strategy — Rapha	202
7.2	Reimagine Top-Down as People-Up — Google	203
7.3	Reimagine Singularity as Mutuality — Lush	204

7.4 Reimagine Metrics as Impacts — Patagonia　206
7.5 Reimagine External as Internal — Victora's Secret　207
7.6 Reimagine What Is as What If — Omeat　208
7.7 Reimagine Homogeneity as Diversity — Chloé　209
7.8 Reimagine the Brand as the Experience — Nike　210
7.9 Reimagine Intellectual Property as Public Property — the FIA　212
7.10 Reimagine Storytelling as Story-Doing — Adidas　213
7.11 Reimagine Time Saved as Time Experienced — Apple　215
7.12 Reimagine Lifestyle as Purposeful Life — Daylesford Organic　216
7.13 Reimagine Outreach as Outlook — National Geographic　216
7.14 Reimagine Digital as Physical — Sweaty Betty　217
7.15 Reimagine the Product as the Byproduct — Tesla　218
7.16 Reimagine Fixed as Circular — The North Face　219
7.17 Reimagine Regenerative Sourcing — Veja　220
7.18 Reimagine Regenerative Manufacturing — Gucci　220
7.19 Reimagine High-Functional & Aesthetic Lifespan — Veilance　221
7.20 Reimagine Multi-Use Afterlife — Massimo Dutti　222
7.21 Reimagine Knowledge, Expertise and Experience — Arc'teryx　223
7.22 Westington, Nuie Design Co & Mad About Land　224

8. HOPE

8.1 Black Swans　232
8.2 Prosperity in Perpetuity — Hope in the Future　233
8.3 Nuie Design Co: Exactly What the North Is Capable Of　237
8.4 Nuie Design Co: A New Approach to Design　239
8.5 Compelling Brand Design: Driving Revenue Growth　242
8.6 Addictive Brand Design: Driving Profit Growth　242
8.7 Emotionalised Brand Design: Driving Enterprise Value　244
8.8 Influence and Impact　245
8.9 Brand Design in Education　246
8.10 Commerce and Creativity　250
8.11 Employment and Enterprise　250
8.12 Geographically, Where Is Growth to Be Found in the Near Future?　253

9. WHAT I HAVE LEARNED FROM OTHERS

9.1	Craig Ford — Billionaire Boys Club	257
9.2	Rachel Thomas — Artist	258
9.3	Jeremy Guard — Founder, Arc'teryx	258
9.4	Erin Summe-Whitehead — Founder, Thandeka Travel	259
9.5	Simon Foxton — Fashion Editor, *i-D* Magazine	260
9.6	Stephen Male — Art Director, *i-D* Magazine	261
9.7	Andy Towne — Vice President, Amer Sports	262
9.8	Tim Delaney — Founder, Leagas Delaney	263
9.9	Sam Pitroda — Indian National Congress	263
9.10	James Curleigh — Global President, Levi's Strauss & Co.	264
9.11	Sir David Brailsford — Team Principal, Team Sky	265
9.12	Lady Carole Bamford — Founder, Daylesford Organic	266
9.13	David Cockcroft — Founder, Blackrose	267
9.14	Ravi Thakran — Founder, Turmeric Capital	268
9.15	Sandy Alexander — Founder, Sandy Dunlop	269
9.16	Sophie Phillips — Co-Founder, FreshBritain	270
9.17	Soldier A — Senior Officer, British Special Forces	271
9.18	Niclas Bornling — Brand Director, Salomon	271
9.19	Roddy Darcy — Creative Director, Arc'teryx	272
9.20	Tony Wood — Nuie Design Co	273
9.21	Micheal Sheard — Father of the Author	274

10. CONCLUSION   278

DEDICATIONS

DAD

"Do something, and something happens."

My father used to say you can't control the talent in the room, but you can control whether you work the hardest. This maxim informed the strong work ethic I have always had. He would also say, *"If you do nothing, nothing happens. Do something, and something happens. So whatever you do, do something, and something will happen."*

While it may seem overly simplistic, there's power in persistent action and positive thinking. If you subscribe to the idea of manifestation and believe in the interconnectedness of our intentions with the universe, you might find that consistent effort creates far-reaching effects. The ripples of change that you send out come back in ways you could never have imagined or hoped for, creating tailwinds ahead of headwinds. In essence, by consistently pursuing your aspirations and visualising your desired outcomes, the universe seems to conspire to bring those dreams to fruition.

Keep doing something, keep manifesting, keep making the change you want to see, and the universe will help design a way to make that come true. Thank you, Dad, RIP.

MUM

"You do you."

Mum, this is me doing me.

SOPHIE

With whom I have been on this journey and of whom the contents of this book is also a life's work and to whom any credit should be deservedly shared, as we have shared our lives and our loves.

HENRY AND DAISY

For some time now, I have only shown you madness. I hope this book shows some method to the madness. Method or madness, there has always been love, and there always will be. You both inspire me every day. Thank you.

RICHARD

Thanks, brother!

HENRY AND SYLVIA

You have made incalculable contributions to the quality of my life. Thank you.

FRESHBRITAIN

It's been 25 years and more than 250 brands, but mostly it's been people. We have had amazing people, and without them we have nothing. Specifically for this book project, I'd like to thank Roberta Galvin, Andy Lipscombe, Steph Thomas, Jack O'Leary, Aziz Cami, Jon Crane, Sion Jones, Jake Parnell-Hogg, Marv Robson, Rhys Hoyte, Ed Harris, Tim Gautrey, Mary Russell and Daisy Phillips-Sheard. Without you, this book wouldn't exist.

EMMA TURNER

The writing companion without whom this would not have happened. Your support and encouragement have been immeasurable and your talent unquestionable. Amazing. Thank you!

MARTIN AND LID PUBLISHING
Thank you for taking a chance.

I'm grateful to all who encouraged this project. What started as seemingly a tangle of wild ideas has been shaped into something I hope will be valuable. I am pulling together conversations that have happened over many years, including with Roddy Darcy from Arc'teryx, Philippe D'aguillon from Simond, Tom and Susie Smith from Westington, John and Lucy Chevenix-Trench from Madresfield, Tony Wood from Nuie, Simon Busby from Bizzarrini, Fran Millar from Belstaff (and now Rapha), Simon Mottram from Rapha, Rebecca Wright from Central Saint Martins (CSM), Roger Wade from BoxFund, David Richards from the Fédération Internationale de l'Automobile (FIA), Phil and Hels from Avonbury and Marcello Bottoli from Boggi Milano. With their help, it has been crafted into something that is hopefully of interest.

CONTEXT — MY STORY

I have had the privilege of working with more than 250 brands, spanning a quarter-century, working with a diverse and wonderful group of people and building value into some of the world's leading companies. There is hopefully some hard-won wisdom here.

I have learned from various professionals and personal connections. These insights cover a wide range of topics, including brand strategy, design principles, business practices and personal growth. Key themes include the importance of simplicity, conviction and authenticity in branding; the value of networking and adding value to others; the power of clear positioning and emotional connection in marketing; the significance of teamwork, with the necessity of a shared vision; and the importance of thinking big, embracing change and continually taking action. These lessons have shaped my approach to brand design, business strategy and personal philosophy.

As a brand designer, I look for and explore the opportunity and solutions that may exist, through seeing things in a different way. I am, remarkably, a northern lad who became an expert in redesigning and repositioning some of the world's most iconic brands and changed the course of some of the biggest brand identities in history.

THE EARLY DAYS: WHERE IT ALL STARTED

My professional journey started early. From the age of 14, I worked with my family of market traders at the John Street Market in Bradford, West Yorkshire. My job was to sell long-sleeve shirts at £4.99 and short-sleeve shirts at £3.99. I'd arrive on Saturday morning to find that the boss had been buying shirts the previous day — an assortment of available styles, patterns and fabrics. Officially, my job was to assist with selling, folding the shirts into bags and managing the till. But instead, I would find myself remerchandising the stand every morning. I knew the patterns of footfall in and around the stand, where the morning traffic flow was and wasn't. I would relocate the most interesting, eye-catching items that my boss had bought and position them along the eyeline of the morning passers-by, observing the patterns of consumption and trying to understand what caught people's eye. Like Warren Buffett, I studied the market.

During my lunch hour, I would again rearrange the stand to optimise sales. Then, in the afternoon, it was sell, sell, sell. It wasn't bad work for a teenager being paid £15 a day. Later, we would compare the takings. The afternoon's sales always doubled the morning's, and I knew early on that I had an eye for these things.

My schooling was in Halifax, West Yorkshire. I went to Ryburn Valley High School, a comprehensive school bad enough to be demolished and rebuilt sometime after I'd left. It was a tough environment, especially for someone small, as I was. I often felt alone and ostracised, attracting significant attention from bullies.

A seemingly innocuous purchase with my market wages was to have a significant, lifelong impact. One day, in year three, I chanced upon a pair of Adidas Lendl Court trainers, and this purchase changed everything. This was definitely the first time these trainers had been worn in Halifax, possibly even Yorkshire. Now, the attention I received changed, from bullying to admiration.

The magic of brands was revealed to me. Owning a pair of these rare (for Yorkshire) Adidas suddenly made me a 'cooler' kid. The trainers gave me credibility. Like a reverse invisibility cloak, they were my very own armour plate. The power of a product to change how you look, feel, are perceived and accepted — the magic of branding

— was revealed to me. Later, my first girlfriend, Lindsey (she looked like a 16-year-old version of the blonde in The Human League), introduced me to Affleck's Palace, a market in nearby Manchester. There, I acquired a taste for vintage Levi's 501 jeans. That further fuelled my understanding of how brands can be truly transformative.

I was among a few other students to get an A grade at A level, the first group in our school's history to reach those lofty academic heights, but oddly, the school discouraged us from applying to polytechnics or universities.

With an A in history, but Es in economics, art and general studies, I was offered a place to read mediaeval poetry at North Staffordshire Polytechnic (now Staffordshire University). I decided I could do better. I chose to pursue another year of study at Huddersfield College while working on a building site to finance my A levels. It was a brilliant year, and I improved my grades enough to be accepted to a product design and business degree programme at the London College of Fashion (LCF).

During my second year at LCF, I worked with my new girlfriend (future wife, co-founder and partner of our brand design company FreshBritain) selling vintage Levi's at London's Camden Market. As part of her dissertation, we would go to an Oxfam distribution depot up in Huddersfield, where everything that hadn't sold in the charity's second-hand shops nationwide was sorted into fabric types before going to Sub-Saharan Africa for distribution. We would buy half a ton of those fabric bales, containing around 600 pairs of jeans, for £150.

From the bale, about 30 pairs would be Levi's, maybe 10 would be Wrangler and perhaps five were Lee Jeans. Everything else was measured and sold at the nearby markets in Halifax, Leeds or Dewsbury. These 500 pairs of random used jeans, at £3 a pair, would give us £1,000–£1,500 in cash per week. We would then go down to London and sell the Levi's, Lee Jeans and Wranglers for around £30 a pair. Every now and again, we'd luck into a vintage pair of the iconic Levi's Big E, either a 501 or 501z, or a Trucker Type 1 or Type 2 denim jacket. We would sell these back to Levi's. The team at Levi's grew to like me. They could see that the young lad from Halifax knew more about their vintage stuff than people in their own company did. They seemed to like the cut of my gib, and they very generously agreed to sponsor the rest of my education. That, in turn, transformed the rest of my life. When I was at Levi's, I worked with a network at *i-D* magazine. In those days, you were either into the *The Face* or *i-D*. For me, the coolest by far was *i-D*. I was on my way.

During my time at LCF, I worked as a student denim designer at Levi's, working on the 501 and Red Tab lines. After university, I was hired by the sneaker company Converse into their UK Brand Communications team. It was at Converse that I started to understand the power of storytelling, and how we are all storytellers — it's just the medium that changes. We are all either telling stories tacitly, through a perceived medium, such as footwear or clothing design, or telling stories more explicitly, through the more direct medium of communication.

I was one of Converse's youngest-ever creative/marketing leads, rising through the ranks fast. A contributing factor may have been the fact that I was prematurely bald. The leadership team didn't really know how old I was, and I kept advancing. By the age of 27, they had made me Creative Director, in charge of footwear selections, clothing, product design and all communications for Converse in Europe, the Middle East and Africa. We were the first to launch products from Japan into Europe: the One Star, the Jack Purcell, the Dr. J, the Weapon and the Skate Star. We were earning a reputation for knowing what to sell and where to sell it. We were also the first brand to significantly invest in music festivals, specifically the backstage area where all the opinion leaders and (nowadays, influencers) hung out. Converse at Reading Phoenix and T in the Park at the height of Britpop was transformational for the All Star.

In 1998, the magazine *FHM Collections* ran a list of the most influential people in world fashion. Ralph Lauren, Phil Knight and Paul Smith made the top five, while Vivienne Westwood came in at number 50. Remarkably, I was listed at 33. Two things struck me about this: I was the youngest and the poorest.

It was likely due in part to that list that I was hired by Alessandro Benetton and Andrea Bonomi, who had set up a new investment fund called 21 Investimenti. They put me on the board of their recently acquired asset Karrimor, with a clear mission to redesign the product and brand for the company's resale. I set about recreating Karrimor as 'The Great British Mountain Company,' which was re-launched with the 1999 campaign, 'Phone In Sick.'

With a fresh approach, a new look and an irreverent attitude, it attracted instant notoriety. The adverts sparked criticism that the message would be taken too literally, with workplaces emptied out as employees headed to the hills. The UK's Advertising Standards Authority announced in week five of the brand launch that they were going to ban the campaign, and the ensuing publicity more than doubled the intended length of the initial 'Phone in Sick' phase. We responded with the same irreverence, changing the tagline on mountaineering shots to 'Go to Work Indecently.'

It certainly got noticed, and instead of selling Karrimor in the anticipated three years, 21 Investimenti were able to sell to Cullinan Holdings of South Africa after just 18 months.

In redesigning Karrimor for a sale, I observed firsthand how private equity influences brands. This project revealed how emotional power can drive valuation multiples and demonstrated how the prospect of an exit shapes both short-term and long-term brand design strategies.

By this time, I had married, my wife had completed her PhD in AI and design at University College London (UCL), and we'd had our first child. With proceeds from the Karrimor deal, we set up our brand agency, FreshBritain, in London.

That was a quarter-century ago. Since then, we have worked with more than 250 brands, ranging from Levi's to LVMH, from Nike to New Balance. We've worked with and shaped some of the world's biggest and most iconic brands. In our first year, we designed the branding for Katherine Hamnett, Kangol and Wolverine. In our second year, we won the Caterpillar account, our first global campaign. Soon after, we won Nike ACG, moving the family to the French Alps to learn snowboarding and live the brand. Back then, I had a method-acting approach to adopting the nature of the prey, becoming a student of the snowboard for Nike ACG, running marathons for New Balance and ultra-marathons for Karrimor, and embracing UVU sports psychology,[1] all to get under the skin of the consumer. I have taken this to the extreme in the pursuit of professional 'product onboarding.' I really pushed my limits while running to the North Pole and losing the end of one of my toes to frostbite. I finished 13th in the race.

Living in the Alps, we were immersed in the culture of the Haute-Savoie. In this region, Salomon sportswear is revered, so it was huge to be asked to redesign the brand. The Salomon project taught us the importance of understanding and repositioning internal culture. On the day we presented our redesign, in the room was the future president of Arc'teryx, the future president of Suunto, the future president of Keen and the future president of Levi's, each of which would become FreshBritain brand design projects.

Our work with Arc'teryx taught us the meaning of place — how a brand's geographic origin can shape personality and identity, weaving into brand ethos. We found the wilderness tranquillity reflected in Arc'teryx's Canadian roots could bring depth and identity to a young brand with very little heritage. Our work with the

---

[1] UVU means 'You Versus You,' describing the moment your body says stop and your mind says carry on. Born out of a passion for athletic discipline, its adherents share a conviction that sport, in its many facets, when pursued by the individual, has the power to change us for the better.

Finnish sporting accessories company Suunto exposed us to the indomitable 'hard to kill' notion of sisu.

After Salomon, we worked for Keen and then Levi's, which brought us full circle. Levi's has been amazing. Our first brand creation project, 'Levi's Made and Crafted,' is now their premium 'Levi's Made' brand. Later, the President of Levi's Global invited me to 'unfuck' the company, which manifested in the 'Live in Levi's' campaign and the company's stock market flotation in 2019.

Along the way, we also worked with Wrangler and had a life-changing meeting with a lovely gentleman called Sandy Alexander. It was Sandy, a branding expert extraordinaire, who taught me the value and impact of emotionalisation of narrative through archetypes. This then led to a decade-long relationship with the London arts and design college Central Saint Martins (CSM), culminating in a knowledge-transfer programme on Brand Design that the business organisation Innovate UK characterised as 'outstanding.' CSM are also our partners on 'The Future of Everything' events and content, which feature heavily in this book. Together, we will create undergraduate and post-graduate educational platforms that take the knowledge gathered over a lifetime of working on the most influential brands and make it openly available. This will hopefully give flight to thousands or tens of thousands of new brands that exist for positive purposes.

This book shares my insights and seeks to decode the secrets of compelling brand strategy design. It unravels the complex weave of graphic design, corporate culture, commercial strategy and storytelling that together create a brand's unique magnetism. It looks at the essential ingredients that are instrumental in forming an emotional brand that transforms.

This is ironically funny coming from someone who couldn't get into CSM as a teenager and had to lie about his maths credentials to get into LCF.

DRIVING POSITIVE SOCIAL CHANGE

Eight years ago, I embarked on a transformative journey to Rwanda with my children. Our mission was to design brands for three United Nations-sponsored, female-led initiatives. It would be an experience that profoundly altered my perspective on the potential of brand design. In that long-troubled East African nation, I was struck by a powerful dichotomy: while Rwanda's past was marred by the disruptive power of male-driven violence, its future was being shaped by women embodying the constructive power of female-driven forgiveness. This stark contrast highlighted the potential for positive change, and I saw an opportunity for brand design to play a crucial role in this transformation.

One of the brands we helped create was Azizi Life. Over the years, this fair trade organisation has significantly improved outcomes for Rwandan women, demonstrating the tangible impact of thoughtful brand design. This served as a testament to how strategic branding can empower communities and drive social progress and was a turning point in my understanding of brand design's potential. I realised that its power extends far beyond making products appealing or boosting sales. Instead, when applied thoughtfully, ethically and responsibly, brand design can transcend its traditional commercial role and become a catalyst for positive empowerment, societal change and progress. This has influenced my approach, encouraging me to seek out projects that both create aesthetic value and contribute to social good. It's a powerful reminder that we can harness our skills as designers to address real-world challenges and make a meaningful difference in people's lives.

The Rwanda project opened my eyes to the broader implications of my work, particularly as I witnessed the decline of the country's tropical mountain landscape and its rich ecosystem, as humankind's everyday actions harm the very places we love.

Over the past 25 years, I've had the privilege of working with many outdoor and sports brands, including Salomon, Arc'teryx, Mountain Equipment, Suunto, Karrimor, TOG 24, Jack Wolfskin, UVU, Kjus, Odlo, Nordica, Atomic, Mountain Force and others. This has provided a unique perspective on the intersection of brand design, consumerism and environmental impact, particularly in mountain ecosystems. Through this journey, I've witnessed firsthand the transformative potential of brand design in addressing societal and environmental challenges, especially climate change. Initially, our work primarily focused on creating compelling brand identities and innovative products. However, as the effects of climate change became increasingly apparent in mountain environments, we recognised the need for a paradigm shift in brand strategy.

We began to understand that brands have the power to influence consumer behaviour and industry practices on a massive scale. By integrating sustainability and environmental responsibility into core brand values, we could leverage the emotional connection between consumers and these outdoor brands to drive positive change and help protect and potentially future-proof the natural world that we love. This involved working with companies to develop initiatives that not only improved product sustainability but also educated consumers about environmental issues. These efforts included designing products with recycled materials, implementing repair and resale programmes and creating marketing campaigns that raised awareness about the impact of climate change on mountain ecosystems.

Moreover, my experience with investment firms, such as Carbon, Venn, Blackrose and Generation Growth Equity (GGE), founded by former US Vice President and environmentalist Al Gore, has demonstrated how financial decisions can be aligned with activist goals. This approach, known as impact investing, has shown that profitability and positive societal change are not mutually exclusive.

By incorporating environmental considerations into investment strategies, we've seen how capital can be directed towards companies that are actively working to mitigate climate change and promote sustainability. This shift in investment focus has, in turn, influenced brand strategies across the outdoor industry, encouraging more companies to adopt sustainable practices and communicate their environmental commitments effectively.

My experience has taught me that brand design, when aligned with a genuine commitment to sustainability and backed by responsible investment, can be a powerful catalyst for positive societal change. By harnessing the influence of beloved outdoor brands, we can inspire millions of consumers to make more environmentally conscious choices and support businesses that prioritise the health of our planet.

Our brand design journey has ranged from sportswear giants like Nike to New Balance, from denim pioneer Levi's to luxury conglomerate LVMH. This diverse experience demonstrates our ability to design brands at scale across various industries. We've proven adept at both reimagining existing brands and creating new ones from the ground up. Notable examples include:

1. Levi's Made and Crafted: A premium line extension.
2. Arquus: A rebrand for Volvo's Defense vehicle division.
3. Madresfield (Mad About Land): A return to regenerative land management.

Our expertise extends beyond traditional branding. In collaboration with Ravi Thakran, then Chairman of LVMH Asia, and the telecom engineer and entrepreneur Sam Pitroda, we advised the Indian National Congress during what would, in April of 2024, be the largest democratic election in human history.

Working with Sam on his book, *Redesigning the World*, expanded my perspective on the potential for large-scale impact. It reinforced the crucial insight that brand design truly has the power to influence positive change on a global scale.

We have shown that it is possible to create brands from scratch, redesign global icons and drive positive outcomes across diverse sectors. This work has reaffirmed my belief that we all have the power to think big and make a significant difference through strategic brand design.

Many people have helped me along the way. They've generously shared their knowledge, insights and experiences, offering guidance and opportunities that have propelled me forward. At times, I've grappled with imposter syndrome, feeling as though I was merely pretending until I could truly succeed. At times, I still feel like I'm 'faking it till I make it,' though perhaps we all are doing so to some extent.

This book is my way of repaying that debt and helping others get that metaphorical hand up from the knowledge, wisdom and experience I've accumulated along the way. Not everyone has the budget to engage the services of cutting-edge creative agencies. This book aims to provide the foundational building blocks of an engaging and successful brand — one that is addictive, valuable and true. Building such a brand calls for developing confidence in your brand strategy and repositioning the debate, not over what to think, but how to think and how to ask the right questions to unlock the most compelling brand vision possible. As a start-up, of course, capital is scarce, and every pound or dollar counts. And while there is never a completely level playing field, the hope is that there is some hard-won wisdom here that meaningfully bridges the knowledge gap between the giant global brands and the young start-ups that hope to one day rival them.

WHY NOW? SERENDIPITY

My father always said, *"you're not more talented than the next person, but you can work harder."* I grew up with the belief that I had to work hard for things to happen. His motto was simple and elegant:

"Do nothing, nothing happens, do something, and something happens, so do something." This book is about doing something.

Recently, a series of serendipitous events have converged, signalling to me that now is the perfect moment to write this book. These interconnected occurrences have not only reinforced the importance of my experiences but have also reminded me of old connections and brought in new ones, in ways I never could have anticipated.

It all began the night after my aunt's funeral. I was in Rutland, smallest county of the country in the East Midlands, and had painted a portrait for a friend's 60th birthday party. While there, I reached out to a Singaporean client who had suffered after losing his wife suddenly. She had grown up in the area and had a tree memorial close by. The simple gesture of leaving flowers led to meeting his sister in law, who was keen to talk through my interactions with her sister. I shared with her my plans to attend a school reunion, where I was due to meet my first girlfriend that introduced me to the vintage Levi's 501s.

In the weeks that followed, I found myself:
1. Offering wisdom to our project director, where elements for the launch were just going wrong, drawing from a 20-year-old experience with Caterpillar, only to receive a call from the very same Caterpillar boss hours later.
2. Launching a gardening brand in Manchester, where against all odds and having tried earlier, I ended up personally connecting with the mayors of both Manchester and Liverpool in an impromptu late night gathering.
3. Painting a portrait of a deceased friend, which led to an unexpected call with two influential women from New York, one of whom had a connection with the gardening brand in Manchester, paving the way for collaboration.

4. Watching a random Netflix film to calm my emotions, only to receive a message linking me to the very actress I had just been watching who was asking for help.
5. Facilitating a meeting where two professionals discovered that they had travelled around South America together 30 years ago, rekindling a long-lost connection.

These seemingly innocuous events have woven together to create a tapestry of interconnectedness; the frequency and intensity of these serendipitous moments suggest that the universe is conspiring to bring people, ideas and opportunities together.

Writing this book now feels not just timely, but necessary, reinforcing the central themes I've always believed in: the power of trust, the importance of authenticity and the value of embracing opportunities. The convergence of all these elements — past experiences coming full circle, new connections forming and old ones rekindling — creates a rich tapestry of stories and insights exploration. Now is the time to weave these threads together, share the lessons learned, and support and inspire others.

In doing so, I am enlisting the help of one of those people I recently met, the sister in law of my Singapore based client, who I first met in Rutland. Serendipity, like Levi's, has come full circle.

A NOTE ON MOMENTS

Just before Christmas 2024, my indomitable editor wrote to me saying that she wanted to hear *"more of my voice"* in the book. Does she just want me to swear more? It's now the 3rd of January, and I awoke this morning with a little revelation. Life is a series of moments. My career has been punctuated by amazing moments.

- Moments of comedy
- Moments of misjudgement
- Moments of clarity
- Pinch-yourself moments
- Mum moments
- Dad moment
- Poignant moments
- Helping-hand moments
- Making it happen moments
- Moments of serendipity
- Moments of light relief

I am throwing these in at the end of the end of each chapter as light relief for making it through each section.

So, as a starter...

"FUCK ME! THERE MUST BE A TAXI DRIVER FROM KAZAKHSTAN DRIVING ROUND BAREFOOT RIGHT NOW."

MOMENTS OF HUMOUR

"NICE SHOES"

I was working for what was then the world's largest surf brand. We were presenting the latest brand vision in Holland. The audience consisted of the head of the brand and various players in his brand and marketing teams.

As it turned out, he was an early-40s Dutch guy, and his team were a harem of very attractive, mid-20s female professionals. They all followed him dutifully into the room. As they walked in, I noticed that the boss was wearing possibly the worst white-patterned, crocodile-skin cowboy boots I'd ever seen. My team saw them as I saw them, and our eyes crossed.

I couldn't help myself and heard myself saying loudly, *"Fuck me! There must be a taxi driver from Kazakhstan driving round barefoot right now."*

The room erupted with laughter. Not the best client-servicing move I've ever made and, in fact, we didn't work with them again.

Relaying the story to a friend who knows me and our direct competitor equally well, he said, *"You know, Bob, that's your problem. Had it been your competitor in the room, he would've just said 'nice shoes' and would be still working with them."*

Undoubtedly true. Oh, well.

"FLAPJACK?"

We used to have a beautiful head office on an estate in the Cotswolds, with a 40-mile view over the Vale of Evesham. When clients arrived, we used to make sure that there was an abundance of drinks, fruits, nuts and snacks laid out on the table.

I suffer from dyslexia, which sometimes manifests as malapropisms. On this occasion, we were presenting to a chemicals business, and the CEO was a rather austere elderly lady who ran the business with a puritanical iron rod. Her team were petrified of her.

I wasn't presenting that day and was watching my team struggle to get the brand vision over the line. The CEO was simply not capable of engaging on an emotional level with the solution. Her team got it, and supported it, but they were so fearful of her their stern leader that none of them was defending our proposal. We were at an anxious impasse.

To break the tension, I decided to hand around some snacks. I turned to Madame CEO to see if she'd like some flapjack. However, what came out of my mouth was...

"Would you like some crack flap?"

Once again, the room erupted. I dissolved into giggles, and we didn't work with them for a long time after that.

LEVI'S

THE PRESIDENT OF LEVI'S GLOBAL INVITED ME TO 'UNFUCK' THE COMPANY, WHICH MANIFESTED IN THE 'LIVE IN LEVI'S' CAMPAIGN AND THE COMPANY'S STOCK MARKET FLOTATION IN 2019.

Design Credit: FreshBritain & Build

THE BRAND NEW FUTURE

LEVI'S

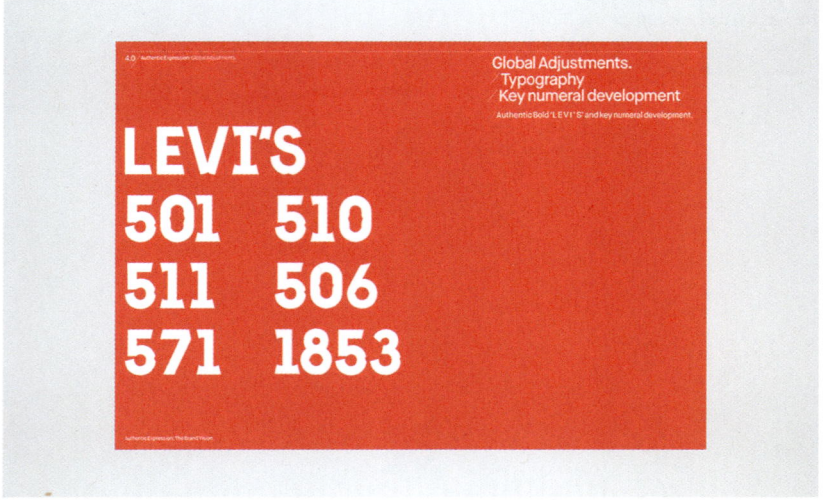

ONE BRAND UNDERSTANDS
THE POWER OF AUTHENTICITY

Design Credit: FreshBritain & Build

CONTEXT – MY STORY

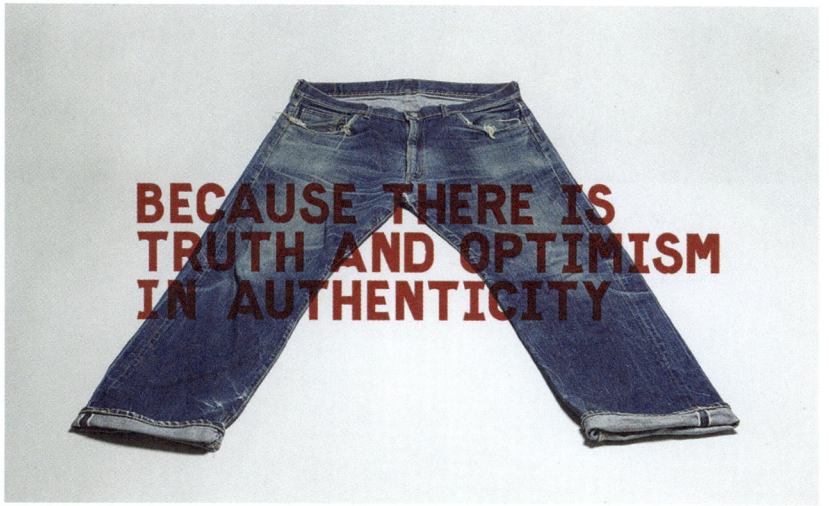

**ABCDEFG
HIJKLMN
OPQRST
UVWXYZ**

Global Adjustments.
Typography

Authentic Bold full character set uppercase.

**BECAUSE THERE IS
TRUTH AND OPTIMISM
IN AUTHENTICITY**

LEVI'S

Photo Credit: Max Cutting

OUR FIRST BRAND CREATION PROJECT, **'LEVI'S MADE AND CRAFTED,'** IS NOW THEIR PREMIUM 'LEVI'S MADE' BRAND.

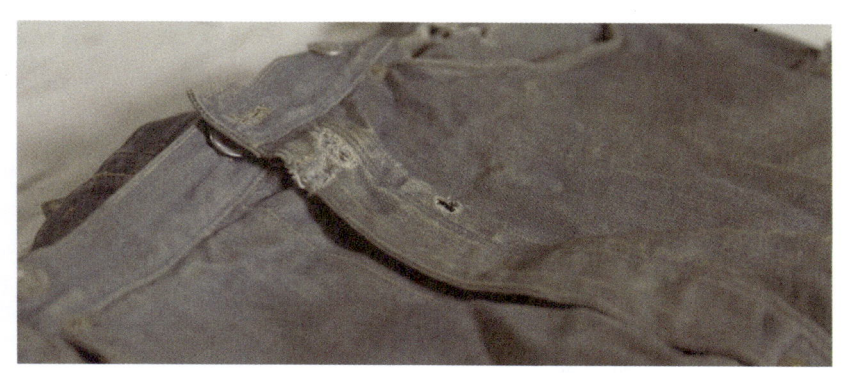

THE BRAND NEW FUTURE

NIKE ACG

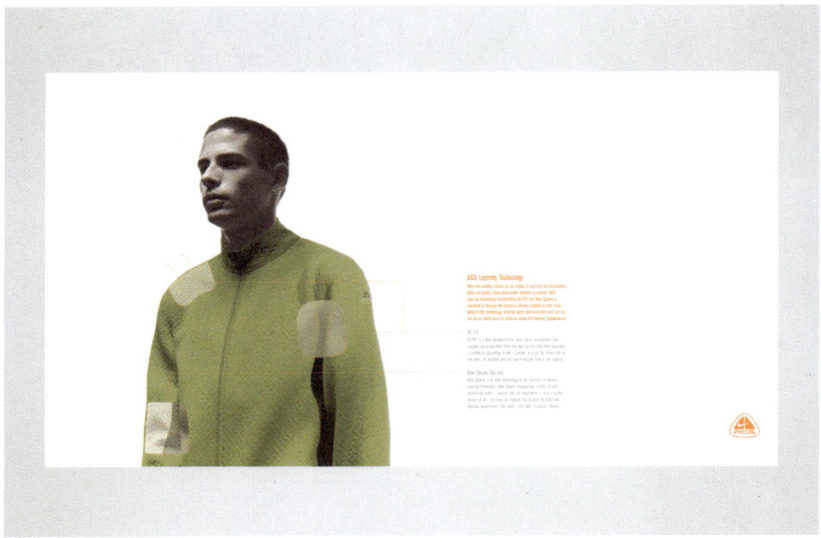

Photo Credit: Neil Stewart

CONTEXT – MY STORY

I HAD A METHOD-ACTING APPROACH TO ADOPTING THE NATURE OF THE PREY, BECOMING A STUDENT OF THE SNOWBOARD FOR NIKE ACG.

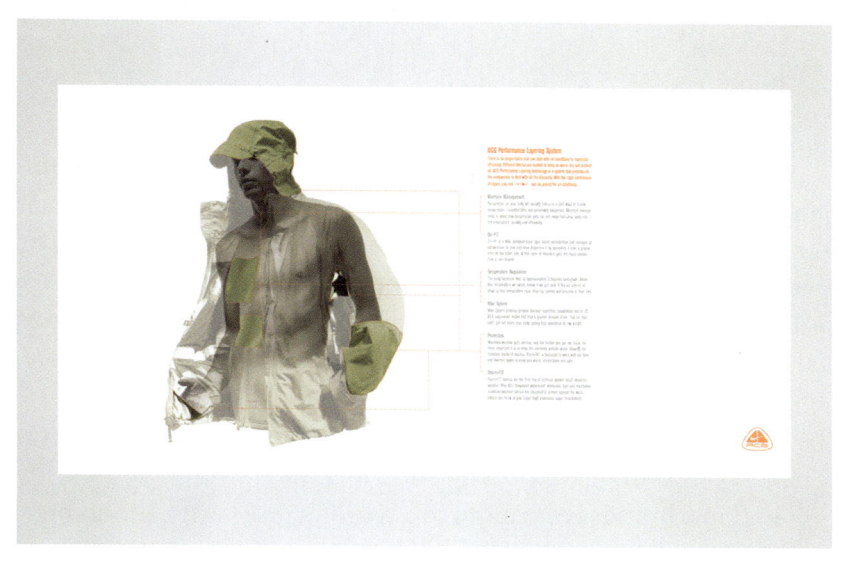

Design Credit: FreshBritain

1. HOW BRANDS WORK

Brands are infused with the connections and interrelated components that contribute to the relationship between a product or service and their consumers. We will examine the power of brands and their sometimes magical impact on business and society. We will present a vision of sustainable prosperity, showing how brands can drive positive change and shape the world we want to see. Together, we will explore:

- The link between company performance and brand Positioning, Personality and Purpose.
- How brands contribute to a nation's prosperity, economic growth and soft power.
- How brands will grow 'beyond zero' (carbon neutrality) and beyond products.
- A sustainable future where brands have a positive regenerative impact.
- How we will shift consumer value systems from being based on 'I own' to 'I do.'
- How brands will become 'story-doers,' not just storytellers.
- How brands will create positive global change.
- How brands can shape the future we want to see.
- How brands can influence areas like politics and policy.

1.1
WHY BRANDS?

Brands have undergone a significant evolution throughout history, reflecting changes in society, technology and consumer behaviour.

In ancient times, people sought answers to the profound questions of existence within the sacred confines of churches and temples. These hallowed spaces were regarded as conduits to the divine, where individuals could explore the purpose of life and uncover insights that held the potential to transform their destinies. During an era when human experience was largely defined by village life or the boundaries of kingdoms, even monarchs sought counsel from religious leaders and oracles to guide their decisions and alleviate the suffering of their subjects during times of disease and famine, striving to ensure prosperity for their realms.

As society advanced, the fabric of civilisation began to shift. Political power emerged, cities expanded, and the world was irrevocably altered by wars and revolutions that reshaped nations and cultures. In this evolving landscape, the collective search for meaning and guidance transitioned from spiritual leaders to political figures. Citizens began to place their hopes and inquiries in the hands of politicians, seeking solutions to the complex challenges they faced.

Fast forward to the present day, and we find ourselves in a moment characterised by what could be termed 'The Escalating Crisis.' This contemporary conundrum reflects not only our pressing global challenges but also a significant shift in where we direct our quest for understanding and purpose. Instead of looking to gods, monarchs or traditional political systems, people are increasingly turning their attention to entities that embody shared values and aspirations — brands.

In this new paradigm, brands have become facilitators of meaning and connection. They offer individuals a sense of agency and allow them to engage with a larger purpose, fostering communities built on decentralised power structures. This shift signifies a profound transformation in how society seeks answers and navigates the complexities of modern life, highlighting the need for alignment with values that resonate deeply in the collective psyche.

The concept of branding has evolved along with this societal shift. Early craftsmen would mark their goods to indicate ownership and quality. However, the modern understanding of brands began to take shape during the Industrial Revolution.

In the 19th century, as mass production became widespread, companies started to differentiate their products through unique packaging and advertising. This era saw the birth of iconic brands like Coca-Cola and Kellogg's, which used distinctive logos and slogans to create brand recognition. The focus was primarily on product features and quality, with brands serving as guarantees of consistency and reliability.

The mid-20th century marked a shift towards lifestyle branding. Companies began to associate their products with aspirational identities, sensibilities and values, moving beyond mere functional benefits. This period saw the rise of brand mascots and characters, as well as the increasing use of mass marketing, including radio and television advertising, to create emotional connections with consumers.

The late-20th century brought about the concept of brand identity, where companies sought to create cohesive product personalities across all touchpoints. This era also saw the emergence of luxury branding, with high-end products and services leveraging exclusivity and status to command premium prices.

The digital revolution of the late-1990s and early-2000s fundamentally changed how brands interact with their customers.

The internet and social media platforms allow for more direct and personalised communication, shifting the balance of power towards consumers. Brands have had to adapt to a more transparent and interactive landscape, where reputation can be made or broken through online reviews, viral content and perceptions of genuine authenticity.

In recent years, brands have increasingly focused on purpose and values. Consumers, particularly younger generations, expect companies to take a stand on social and environmental issues and create a sense of shared community. This has led to the rise of cause-related marketing and corporate social responsibility initiatives as integral parts of brand strategy.

The current brand landscape is characterised by personalisation and data-driven marketing. Advanced analytics and artificial intelligence allow businesses to understand their impact and tailor their messaging and offerings to individual consumers in ways not previously possible. Additionally, the rise of influencer marketing and brand ambassadors has created new channels for brand associations and promotion, blurring the lines between personal recommendations and sponsored content.

Looking ahead, brands are likely to continue evolving in response to technological advances, changing consumer expectations and vast global challenges. The increasing importance of sustainability, the growth of the metaverse, ever-evolving societal values, patterns of global economic growth and the potential of technologies like augmented reality are just a few factors that will shape the future of branding.

This book reflects the impact of an increasingly empowered consumer base, driving the change they want to see and shaping the future they want to inhabit and the brands they want to pass on to the next generation.

1.2
WHY NOW?

This book is based on years of conversations with industry leaders from various fields. These discussions revealed important truths about business, theory and ideology.

In *The Brand New Future*, I will explain how climate change is catalysing the shift 'beyond zero,' why now, why Gen Z will be the ones to get on with it, how brands can help them, and why there is still reason for hope.

CLIMATE CHANGE: WHY NOW, AND WHY US?

Many still underestimate the urgency of climate change. It is becoming increasingly clear that it poses an existential threat, with global consequences, ratcheting up tensions even in stable regions by exacerbating social and economic problems, as we saw happen with the COVID-19 pandemic.

Over the decades, I've designed for leading outdoor brands, and I've witnessed first-hand how climate change impacts their operations. I have seen the struggle with the changing landscapes; mountains, like oceans, serve as Earth's early warning system. These environmental shifts affect not just our clients but also our own business.

Here's why this demands immediate attention.
The escalating crisis:
- Temperatures are reaching new extremes
- Droughts are increasingly severe
- Weather patterns are becoming more erratic
- Storms are intensifying in ferocity
- Flooding and wildfires are becoming more frequent and intense

The natural world is shrinking:
- Ice packs are diminishing
- Sea ice is retreating
- Glaciers are receding
- Environmental stability is deteriorating

The looming consequences:
- More pollution
- Accelerated species extinction
- Widespread food insecurity
- Deepening poverty
- Increased and larger-scale migration
- Greater global unrest

There's an element of self-interest, but it's crucial that we consider the bigger picture. A key component of this is reimagining growth. How can we grow brands sustainably in this changing world?

An additional answer to the question 'Why us?' is 'Why not us?' Who is going to act it if not we ourselves? We're all capable of examining our own conscience and asking this within our own spere of influence and expertise. 'What can I do?' and 'How can I can act?' Multiply that by eight billion citizens of Planet Earth, and we are on our way...

A beneficial caveat: It is now commonly accepted that on the battlefields of the Second World War, only one in 10 soldiers actually shot to kill. That means that only 10% of combatants shaped the outcome of a battle. The logical extension is that we only need a tipping point of 800 million on Earth to influence the outcome for eight billion.

To start any movement, first we need a madman and a first follower. First follower, anyone?

In the context of this book, to start, we have to understand how brands grow. What are the conventional routes for growth, and how do you get there?

In brand design, there is a simple formula for growth: You create a compelling brand identity. That is, an understanding of your positioning that will bring people to your brand. This will generate turnover. Then, you need people to stay, developing loyalty through creating an episodic and serial relationship with your consumer, forging an emotional connection so it remains their brand of choice, driving profit.

The three elements to bring together for conventional brand design are Positioning, Personality and Purpose to transform outcomes.

POSITIONING

The components of positioning are really important. A common mistake is trying to have as broad a base as possible to attract as many consumers as possible. As it stretches its positioning across as many geographies and/or products as possible, a brand becomes more opaque and less logical. It is rendered less identifiable and understandable. I urge brands to focus and thoughtfully narrow their positioning in order to broaden their appeal. It's about finding where in the world the brand occupies.

The second part is identifying the brand's authority. This is the compelling expertise or knowledge that the brand has to personify in that sector.

The third factor is the 'reason to believe' — what brings consumers to the brand, linked to authority. Why does that brand have a rightful position in that sector and become the product of choice/desire?

Our work with the French outdoor gear company Salomon in 2007 is an excellent case study that brings all these elements together. This project centred on getting the positioning of the brand right so that people would come to it.

In 2006–07, Salomon had been sold by Adidas to a Finnish holding company called Amer. Although it was turning over

£300 million, following multiple sales, the company had lost its way and its confidence.

Early in our work with the brand, I was taken to a file-filled room that company founder George Salomon would often escape to. Intrigued, I asked about the files and was told they contained more than 8,000 patents. This was four times the number of patents held by Adidas, which had just sold Salomon, and twice as many as held by NASA. This was an extraordinary amount of innovation, entirely focussed on soft and hard mountain sport goods. Salomon operated on both the front side of the mountain, in formalised skiing, such as the Olympic Games ski races, but also on the backside, in snowboarding and off-piste skiing. And it covered every season of the year, with the growth of trail running and rock climbing. It was also a brand that truly existed in the French Alps, with more than 1,000 employees who lived and worked on the mountains, designing products for mountain sports innovation since 1947.

Understanding these elements provided a simple positioning: Salomon, the Mountain Sports Company. This was a clear, deep-rooted, undeniably authentic identity. It was about moving it away from a lifestyle proposition and saying, 'This isn't lifestyle, it is life.'

Sometimes, my role is to show what is extraordinary and unique, which can be easily lost when you're deeply embedded within the brand. Salomon had lost touch with the fact that they live in one of the most beautiful places on Earth, create wonderful products and have an amazing culture of innovation and communal spirit and support. We moved Salomon back to their essential truth — they were not a lifestyle brand, but an innovation and specialised tech company — narrowing the pitch to broaden the appeal.

That repositioning enabled the company to see and make choices (such as stop web surfing, start trail running). Salomon transformed themselves, leveraging their rich patent archive. Their turnover grew from £300 million in 2008 to more than a billion pounds in revenue 10 years later, with a significant proportion of that due to trail running. This was largely attributable to pivoting the brand positioning around mountain sports. They didn't need the big ad campaign; it was about getting the positioning right and anchoring in the truth of who they were and are. In military terms, we helped them win the battle without firing a shot.

PERSONALITY

Constructing a brand's personality is the secret behind creating a brand's addictive pull — embedding the emotional effect in the consumer for a lifelong connection. It answers the fundamental question, 'What is the emotional effect we're designing?' What do you want your customers to feel when they interface with your brand, whether through wearing a product, using an item or seeing a piece of communication? The brand values can be rational: they can talk to the product, or emotional: they talk to a brand's character. The rational values shape why we need that product, while the emotional values help shape why we want it. Adding a high level of charisma is the aim: designing an idea, articulating what the brand stands for and creating leaders we can follow.

In 2011, I worked hard to create a personality for a superbrand from Vancouver, Arc'teryx, a high-performance outdoor equipment company offering leading innovations in climbing, skiing and alpine technologies. This centred on designing a compelling and addictive personality and building emotional connections of trust — that this was a brand whose magic was in their products. This was a brand that lived in balance with nature, which consumers developed addiction to through the creation of place and developing trust through craftsmanship. Their nearest competitor, The North Face, is all about conquering nature ('Never Stop Exploring'). If you want to conquer nature, consume The North Face. If you want to live in balance with nature, then choose Arc'teryx. This created the addictive and compelling personality that fuelled three-fold profit growth.

PURPOSE

Purpose is becoming more and more important post-COVID-19. As we navigate through more crises, be they financial, environmental or geopolitical, purpose takes on the dimension of morals and missions, of values and culture. Purpose resonates more with the younger consumer, who has greater concern for ethical positioning, community values and longer-term sustainability and environmental protection.

With Volvo Defense, we worked to turn the company from a diesel truck maker to a developer of mobility defence systems. The purpose centred on the provision of agile NATO defence systems as forces for good around the world, helping create 72% growth. Aligning the mission and the purpose for Volvo Defense, aiming for 'more mission,' helped increase their enterprise value by €200 million.

It was a privilege to work with iconic footwear brand Dr. Martens, to get their Positioning, Personality and Purpose aligned around the concept of rebellious self-expression. This took them from a €90 million turnover, grappling with a double-digit decline, to a €3.5 billion flotation in 11 years.

The key learning here is that growth happens when you design and align brands properly. It's an understanding that when you own a 'goods' company, up to 20% of its market capital is derived from its brand value. If you're a services business, that can rise to 40%. Yet most companies don't understand the levers they have to pull to maximise brand value around Positioning, Personality and Purpose. Scale this up to an entire economy — the sum of its goods and services and by extension the sum of its brands — and those in charge of macroeconomies surely need to understand brand value and the responsibilities that come with it.

Over the last five years, the conversations have been changing. There's growing awareness that brands must evolve beyond simply selling more products to become drivers of positive, sustainable change in society and the environment. I have seen the shift in consumer values and evolution of product placement and brand communication, starting with rational product advertising. We're seeing a move towards more sophisticated brand advertising, emotionalising the brand proposition, connecting with the consumer and progressing to persuasive community-based communication. With the rise of internet use and social media, we have created campaigns and communication strategies that generate like-minded communities and, in turn, these communities generate commerce.

And now, we're moving into an era of impactful communication typified by the awareness and meaning behind Patagonia. The outdoor apparel maker's simple statement that their profits are going into a trust, and Earth is their 'only shareholder,' is powerful, emotive and aligned with evolving consumer values.

Contrast this with what we have seen over time. Seventy-five years ago, Chesterfield cigarette ads featured the future president of the United States, B-movie actor Ronald Regan, sending cancer sticks to his family and friends at Christmas. Some 45 years later, his wife Nancy fronted the 'Just Say No' war-on-drugs campaign. We look back now and think, 'How could they?'

Today, most companies are still focused on increasing brand awareness to encourage more (and more) consumption. Very few have crossed into the era of impact communication. They're in the brand sector and the persuasive sector. Put yourselves in the shoes of someone 75 years from now, at the turn of the next century. They'll look back on this time and say, *"When the world was on fire, what did brands do?"* Future generations will view the continued emphasis on conspicuous consumption quite negatively.

We have the opportunity to change this, to be on the right side of history, as we are ultimately judged by our grandchildren. We can change the brand strategy approach from conventional brand communication (community and persuasion) to more impactful

communication. It's time to address the harder questions and manage the greater challenges. To do that, we need to redress our critical thinking and start to consider the unthinkable:
- How do we go and make less stuff?
- How do we manage to sell less stuff but continue to grow?
- How do businesses grow while reducing their environmental impact?
- How can we redesign growth?
- How do we re-educate?
- How can we redesign the enterprise?

How can we redesign brand growth to be more sustainable as we move from 8 billion people on this planet to a projected population of 11 billion by the end of the century?[2] We've added a billion people in just the past 12 years. The implications for the planet, and humankind's welfare, are huge. The risks and opportunities of our population boom and parallel resource crisis depend largely on decisions we've not yet made, including how we tackle climate change.

Brands must evolve beyond simply selling products to becoming drivers of positive, sustainable change in society and the environment. We need to move production towards carbon-neutral, being ecologically progressive and environmentally responsible through managing resource depletion and mitigating environmental damage. Not just because it's the right thing to do, but because Generations Y and Z are demanding change, asking that we use our collective knowledge, intelligence and experience to bring about positive, long-lasting change.

We need to reimagine the future of brands. And to do this, we first must consider growth, because the challenge of growth is the big issue.

---

[2] The United Nations declared 15 November, 2022, the 'Day of Eight Billion' to mark its estimate that humanity had reached that staggering population milestone. While UN demographers project that world population will exceed 10 billion this century, other research predicts an even earlier peak.

Bad growth is socially obsessive. Individual status is defined by how much we have — how many bedrooms we have, how many holidays we go on, how many cars we own. Here in the UK, our nation's standing is driven by metrics of GNP and GDP growth, whether we are in the G20 or G9 economic blocs, and how our growth rate compares with our European neighbours.

From a commercial business perspective, the metrics that matter revolve around growth: profit growth, revenue growth, market share growth. Growth is economically compulsive, but it can also be ecologically regressive, leading to destruction, destabilisation and the degradation and degeneration of our resources.

In a pivotal year for democracy, around 1.5 billion people went to the polls as significant elections took place in more than 50 countries, which between them hold almost half the world's population. Having so many elections in 2024 offered unique insight, with significant geopolitical implications as voters around the globe decided who holds the reins of power (for better or worse), and we were swept along with the changing tides of political and social trends. One common factor is our politicians' promises of economic growth to support their campaign policy pledges, feeding the cycle of addiction to unsustainable growth.

It falls to us, as consumers and as brand designers and shapers of culture, to create the space for our politicians to move into. We need to lead the reimaging of brands so we can deliver on reimaging growth, repositioning consumption, production and ultimately our values. We need to find the sweet spot of future growth that is above the economic threshold for purposeful, sustainable life but below the ecological threshold of irreversible damage and environmental decline. It's imperative that we respond to motivational change from our consumers as we move through future generations. It means recognising the shift from my generation of 'status seekers,' striving for more and showing off our wealth... to Generation Y, which is social media-obsessed and 'content seeking,' telegraphing how much better they were at what they do, how much more connected they are with nature and their communities... into Gen Z, who are redefining our perspectives around propose, how we live our lives, the rules we live by and how we spend our time.

Slowly, we can see consumers changing and transitioning, becoming less defined by what they own and more by what they do, leading us to the key to the future of brand growth.

As such, the call to action for brands and consumers is to:
- Reimagine growth, consumption and production
- Design brands to operate within sustainable limits
- Create space for political change by shifting consumer behaviour

When consumers are less and less defined by what they own and more and more by what they do, this will reshape patterns of consumption away from products and towards experiences. As such, brands will have to find new pathways to growth that do not rely products. When this is the profitable norm, our leaders will have no option but to fill the space with policies designed to encourage these new pathways as the new route to raising tax revenues. Simple.

VOLVO / ARQUUS

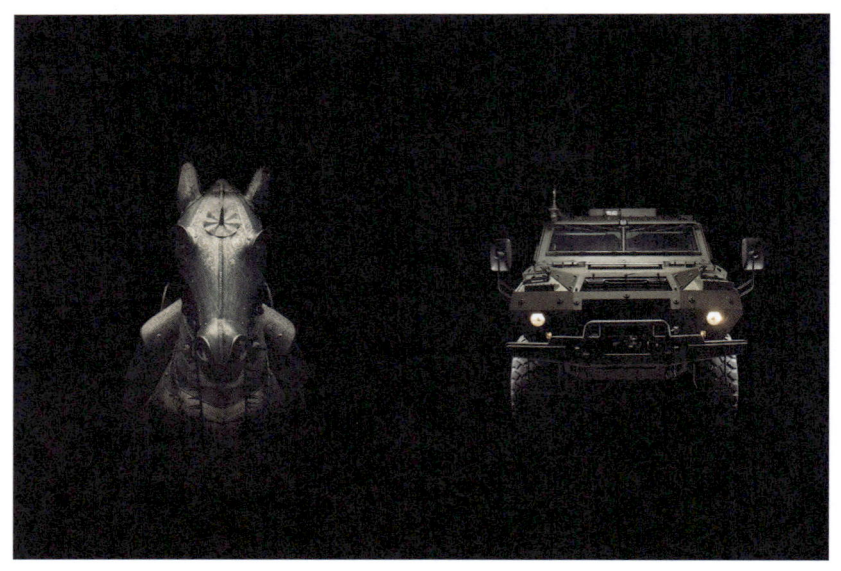

Photo Credit: Jim Yeomans

ALIGNING THE MISSION AND THE PURPOSE FOR VOLVO DEFENSE, AIMING FOR 'MORE MISSION,' HELPED INCREASE THEIR ENTERPRISE VALUE BY €200 MILLION.

VOLVO / ARQUUS

Photo Credit: Jim Yeomans

HOW BRANDS WORK

1.3 PROSPERITY AND POPULATION

Brands exist to satiate consumer demand; consumer demand is driven by 'need' and 'want.' By far the biggest impact on consumer demand is sheer numbers. More people means more demand. More population means more products. More products mean more production, more landfill, more wastewater, more CO2. Control population, and we start to control the impact of consumption and production.

All we need to know is here — written in these numbers is the code for the future of the world:

1 1 1 4
1 1 2 5
6 0 3 5

The top row was roughly the world's population code at the turn of the 21st century:
- 1 billion people living in North America
- 1 billion people living in Europe
- 1 billion people living in Africa
- 4 billion people living in Asia

The middle row is roughly the world's population code by the year 2040:
- 1 billion people living in North America
- 1 billion people living in Europe
- 2 billion people living in Africa
- 5 billion people living in Asia

The bottom row is roughly the world's wealth code for 2040:
- 60% of the world's disposable income will be spent in Asia
- 3.5 billion newly middle-class Asians will spend $3 trillion on brands

The first key observation here is that of the 7 billion people in the top row, 1 billion live in extreme poverty. This means:
- No food source
- No fuel source
- No water source

This drives population growth, as families living in extreme poverty need:
- Two children to get the food
- Two children to get the fuel
- Two children to get the water

The second key observation here is the importance of the stability between the first two columns of the second row. From the top row to the bottom row, the numbers don't change — they remain '1.'

This is because from 2025 to 2040, the projected population in North America and Europe remains at 1 billion per continent. In other words, it has stabilised. The key difference between North America and Europe, where population growth is stable, and Africa and Asia, which each add a billion souls, is that most of the daughters of North America and Europe are educated, unlike in Asia and Africa.

The key to stabilising global population growth is to educate the daughters of Asia and Africa. Education reveals alternatives to solutions for the provision of food, fuel and water, other than more babies.

If we act now, we should be able to stabilise global population at 12 billion by the end of the century.

An interesting note here is that the UK historically runs at 1% of the global population. This means the UK population should stabilise at 120 million by 2099. We will need a national infrastructure programme akin to that of today's Japan — widely seen as the best in the world — to support a population of 120 million.

The third key observation is the importance of Asia. For a national economy, company or brand to win globally in the 21st century, it must win in Asia. Asia is global. We must understand the needs, wants, desires and opportunities of Asia.

Asia is transitioning from Earth's manufacturer to Earth's marketplace. Roughly speaking, Asia is:
- 48 countries
- 11 major religions
- 2,000 languages

To unlock Asia will require talent with deep cultural, economic and personal ties. Interestingly, in the UK, we have 8 million second-generation Asians with just those ties. Time for a Ministry for Asia, anyone?

As we consider the future of growth and prosperity, we must consider this vast market.

As brand designers, we used to obsess about trends in New York, Chicago and LA. Now, it's Jakarta, Hanoi and Colombo. Why? Because by 2040, the combined middle-class population of Vietnam, Indonesia and Sri Lanka will exceed that of North America.

1.4

BRAND STRATEGY

Brand strategy touches many different facets of a brand or a company. It is the intersection of communication and design. It's the nexus of graphic design, product design and commercial strategy design. It encompasses storytelling, emotional touchstones and corporate culture. It's really the epicentre of how a company orients itself and uses its brand to interface with the consumer.

Defining brand strategy can be catalysed by four questions:
1. What is our purpose?
2. What are our beliefs?
3. What are our values?
4. What is our story?

We can find the answers to those questions by looking at the consumer and defining how they make their decisions. We know that 85% of human decision-making is subconscious. Theoretically, it follows that 85% of human consumption is driven by our subconscious mind. The reason is that we feel more quickly than we think. We feel that we want something seven times faster than we're thinking about whether we can afford it.

When designing a brand, and when creating a brand strategy, we have to do so in the knowledge that we're actually designing a story that should already exist in the consumer's subconscious. It should be a narrative that not only exists but that they want to be a part of.

Brand strategy and design serve as the foundation for a company's identity. When executed effectively, they possess the remarkable ability to transform intangible creativity into something tangible. Compelling brand design attracts people to both the brand and the company, ultimately driving turnover as more customers take note, engage and make purchases.

An addictive brand design evolves the relationship between the brand and its customers, making it episodic and serial in nature. This transformation extends the relationship from core products to non-core offerings, thereby increasing profitability.

Creating an emotional connection through compelling brand design drives value. When a company aims to increase its value, it typically focuses on developing a financial profile oriented around value creation, establishing a fundamental value proposition for customers and aligning with the macroeconomic context. Adding an emotional layer to these strategies can 'emotionalise the multiple' — the factor applied to a company's profit or revenue to determine its value.

In essence:
1. Compelling design drives revenue by attracting customers.
2. Addictive design increases profit by fostering ongoing relationships. Moving design emotionalises the multiple, potentially increasing the company's valuation.

These elements combine to significantly impact enterprise value — the overall worth of the company. In economic terms, a company's brand is its ability to sell more and command higher prices. And those with a strong brand can actually shift demand. For example, there was virtually no demand for electric vehicles but high demand for Tesla's electric cars. There is low demand for computer tablets but high demand for iPads. Thus, successful branding can break away from the economies of their market and form their own.

By focusing on these aspects of brand strategy and design, companies can have a transformational effect on their market position and financial performance.

Aggregate the sum of an economy's brands, and the same truth can also have a transformational effect on the economic performance and global position of a nation.

1.5 HUMANS AS STORYTELLERS

If 85% of our decision-making occurs in the subconscious, it's worth some conscious thought about our subconscious!

What is it about human evolution that makes us natural born storytellers? Where do these stories live inside us, and how can we engineer brand design to affect the subconscious?

We often consider it an immutable fact that humans are the only species on Earth that tells stories. Our ability to create and share narratives sets us apart from our closest relatives, such as chimpanzees. For instance, chimps in Rwanda are unaware of their counterparts across the lake in Tanzania. This lack of awareness beyond their immediate community limits their ability to create unified meaning and organise on a larger scale (outside of Planet of the Apes!).

Humans have evolved differently. Since our ancestors first gathered around campfires and drew pictographs on cave walls, we've been telling stories and creating shared meanings. This ability allows us to connect with people who don't share our geography. A Roman Catholic in West Yorkshire may have meaning systems in common with one in Uganda, just as an American in New York shares cultural touchstones with an American in California.

Our storytelling ability has enabled us to build civilisations, religions, companies, nations and even brands. It's how we evolve as a species, as cultures and as consumers. From childhood bedtime stories to films and TV shows, books, plays and songs, we consume narratives constantly. The stories that repeat become archetypally ingrained in our memories and subconscious, which we can then leverage to create brand stories or other cultural narratives.

Interestingly, similar stories and archetypes emerge in different parts of the world, among people who have no direct contact. This phenomenon is underpinned by the universality of human emotions. While I may share little in common with someone in Helsinki, we both experience happiness, sadness, desire and disgust. The emotional language is the same, even if the triggers may differ culturally.

For example, we can both be inspired by a rebel narrative — someone who takes from the few to give to the many. In Anglo-Saxon tradition, this might be Robin Hood; in Scandinavia, it would be Leninakan; and in North America, Geronimo. While the specific character may change depending on the culture, the narrative structure and emotional impact remain consistent.

As we build the Positioning, Personality and Purpose of brands, we must be aware of these universal human emotions and the power of storytelling. If 85% of our decision-making occurs in the subconscious, tapping into these shared narratives and emotions can be a powerful tool for brand design and communication.

But… sometimes, we're still capable of misjudgements.

"I TOLD HIM NOT TO BE SO STUPID — NO ONE WOULD EVER WEAR SOMETHING CALLED 'MOUNTAIN WAREHOUSE.'"

MOMENTS
OF MISJUDGEMENT

"DEAD IN ANYTHING ELSE"

While serving as Creative Director at Converse in Europe, I was always trying to inspire the creative team in the US to bigger and better things. To push the envelope, so to speak. On occasion, I'd send them conceptual creative work that was never meant to see the light of day, intended only to nudge the internal team into new creative space.

This was the '90s, and sadly, within months of each other, Kurt Cobain, the lead singer of Nirvana, and River Phoenix, the My Own Private Idaho actor, had died.

Both had spent their last hours wearing Converse.

In my irreverent enthusiasm, I thought that a campaign titled 'Would never be seen dead in anything else' would be a fitting tribute.

Needless to say, my US bosses did not agree, and while I didn't get sacked (which I probably should have), I did get strongly reprimanded.

Not for the first time, my youthful exuberance had got the better of my judgement.

"BE PREPARED"

When we were rebranding the Scout Movement, I wanted to force a real appraisal of the scouting brand. I wanted to show that fearless tolerance and relentless kindness were not just soft values but in fact cool values.

I instructed my team to research the alumni of the scout movement and find me the most famous and coolest members.

We hit the jackpot when we discovered that The Rolling Stones' Keith Richards used to be a scout.

I presented a concept to the UK Scout Association's board: 'It's the Scout in him that's kept him alive.' To wit, on the occasions when ol' Keef must've been close to death, and didn't do that last line of coke, it was the little scout in him that stopped him.

Funnily enough, they didn't go with it.

Sometimes what's brilliant for you isn't entirely brilliant for the other guy.

"DON'T BE SO STUPID"

When I was on the board of Karrimor as the company's Creative Director, I had many fun conversations with the Retail Director.

When the brand was sold, we discussed what we were going to do next. I was going to set up an agency with my wife, and he was going to take on the Karrimor stores but rebrand them.

When he told me the name of the rebrand, I told him not to be so stupid — no one would ever wear something called 'Mountain Warehouse.'

Today, 25 years on, having done just that, he is one of the richest men in the country.

2. CONVENTIONAL BRAND DESIGN

2.1 BRAND DESIGN DELIVERING GROWTH

As we have touched on, on a macro level, using the three Ps (Positioning, Personality and Purpose) can be a driver of growth in turnover, profit and value. Brand Design can turn the intangible Brand Creativity into very tangible Business Growth.

Now, let's unpack this on micro level. Using examples from my brand experience, we can identify which levers to pull to optimise brand performance.

We will start with brand positioning, exploring its constituent parts: brand world, brand authority and brand essence.

Get this positioning right, and the world will understand you. Some will walk away, but more and more will walk towards you, driving revenue growth.

2.2 BRAND DESIGN DELIVERING REVENUE

POSITIONING: BRAND WORLD

Brand world refers to the sector that the brand resides in. Mastering the space the brand inhabits requires a detailed understanding of the world that you are operating in.

Inov-8 exercise wear has a strong trail running business in the UK. Across the pond, in the US, they had a strong business in CrossFit. It wasn't clear what their world was — trail running or CrossFit. Did CrossFit influence trail running, or was it the other way around? Neither, in fact. But what was certain was their unique proposition, which enabled them to inhabit both those worlds: their footwear's tenacious grip. Their grip enables runners to barrel fiercely down mountains but also to train fiercely on the multiple surfaces that exist in a CrossFit gym. This meant that we could find the common purpose and occupy a world that brought these elements together: 'All Terrain.' We identified their world as all terrain performance, a well-defined world for us to occupy. This brings real clarity to Inov-8's proposition. Our new brand proposition, 'The All Terrain Running Company,' focused on the core product differentiator, 'grip,' that in turn delivers 'fearlessness' to the consumer.

Salomon, as we've described, was repositioned as an innovation and tech company for mountain sports — one of the few brands that occupies 'both sides' of the mountain. Although they had been spending millions on sponsorships with big-name athletes like Hermann Maier,[3] their big-volume business was actually happening on the backside of the mountain, where athletes could be partnered with for £30,000, not £30,000,000. This meant that we could alter their economic model while defining their world as mountain sports and mountain sport innovation, bringing a higher degree of focus to the company.

Brand positioning is crucial for long-term success. Many once-prominent companies have faded into obscurity due to a narrow understanding of their market or sector. Consider these cautionary tales:

---

[3] Austrian alpine ski racer Hermann Maier, born in 1972, is an Olympic gold medalist and World Cup champion. Nicknamed 'The Herminator,' he ranks among the greatest downhill racers in history.

1. Polaroid: They defined themselves by instant film rather than instant imagery, missing the digital revolution.
2. Blockbuster: By remaining focused on in-store movie rentals, they failed to recognise the shift towards at-home, on-demand entertainment.
3. Mail-order giants: Despite having robust infrastructure (credit systems, warehousing, fulfilment), a huge existing audience), they clung to printed catalogues, overlooking the potential of e-commerce.

These examples highlight a common pitfall: defining one's business too narrowly and not future-proofing by moving with more agility and sensing the direction of the market. The mail-order companies, for instance, had all the components to become the next Amazon. Yet they saw themselves as catalogue retailers, obsessed with the printed book, rather than providers of convenient home shopping experiences.

This is a stark reminder of the importance of evolving your strategy to understand the perspectives of your world.

Companies must:
1. Regularly reassess their core purpose and value proposition.
2. Stay attuned to technological advances and shifting consumer behaviours.
3. Embrace a broader, more adaptable vision of their role in the market.

The brand world is broad and open, and it is distinct from a brand lens that's narrow and precise. (More on that later.)

In today's rapidly evolving business landscape, maintaining a flexible and forward-thinking perspective is essential for survival and growth. Companies that successfully anticipate and adapt to change are better positioned to thrive in the long run.

Dyson is an excellent example of a brand that has future-proofed its perspective of the world. Is Dyson a vacuum company or an airflow company? Is their world vacuums or airflow?

Very cleverly, they realised theirs was the world of airflow, which took them into new products and new sectors. Dyson could have been successful as just a hoover company, but their airflow positioning made them a pioneering multinational tech giant with a range of vacuum cleaners, hair care devices, air purifiers, humidifiers, fans and clothes dryers.

A thorough understanding of your world allows you to consider and better envision your future. Branding is what consumers think you are — what's in their subconscious and what their gut feeling is when they see your logo, think about you or use your product. Therefore, when we think about brand positioning, it's important to take external counsel. Ask people what their current belief systems are to gauge their subconscious understanding of your product in the wider brand world.

Being conscious of how you are perceived is important, but it's not as important as how you react to it. This is evident in The North Face and Timberland — ostensibly rugged, durable outdoor brands geared towards cold-weather activity. In the late 1980s and into the '90s, both were worn by New York drug dealers who peddled their goods on wind-blown street corners. A jacket to keep you warm and conceal the dope (and likely a handgun) and boots to keep you warm so you can stay outside, running your corner. Both products were bought in mass quantities from Paragon Sports, a sprawling, 117-year-old sporting goods store on West Broadway. They became totemic in urban American culture as they migrated from those street corners into hip-hop.

The North Face saw it happening and decided not to lean into it, staying true to their identity. Sure, they basked in the reflective glow of being adopted by that culture, but they didn't actively target it. Timberland's approach was different. They saw it happening and actively targeted it. In doing so, the brand lost credibility and market share, ultimately leading it into choppy waters.

The North Face reacted in the right way, understanding that their core world was the great outdoors, exploration and testing one's limits. They didn't turn away from their earned identity but actively decided against leaning into urban adoption, effectively leveraging the economics this created for them.

Timberland, in creating campaigns and products that actively targeted urban America, had missed an essential brand truth. The reason hip-hop culture initially adopted Timberland was that it provided an aspirational refection of another world. It wasn't a mirror image of the consumer's own world. Timberland did not understand that a brand is not a mirror to the consumer; it should be an aspirational reflection. As soon as they became a mirror and not an aspirational refection, they came unstuck.

They mistook their world, trying to cater to new urban consumers without authenticity, and in the process neglected their core customer base.

POSITIONING — AUTHORITY

Every brand must have a point of authority, some reason that gives them credibility and relevance in the marketplace. In examples from major brands, such as Levi's, Daylesford Organic and Adidas, we see companies wielding authority through their rich heritage, innovative practices and guiding principles.

Within positioning, authority is important because it's the credible reason why a brand exists. It's the critical brand action that justifies your agency to speak and act within the market. It defines your compelling knowledge, expertise and reason to be there.

A good example globally is Levi's. The denim pioneer is the best in the world at designing elegant decay, giving prominence to their historical and cultural significance. The more you wear them, the more it reveals the character of you, what you do and your life in those jeans. And that's increasingly powerful. The brand's authority comes from the fact they've done that for more than a century and a half. When we look at the world's oldest pair of jeans in the Levi's archive — a '9Rivet' pair dating to before 1875 — it contains the biography of the miner who wore them, revealed through the fabric's patina, wear and tear. We can see on the garment where he placed his wallet and his tools, like a California gold rush Shroud of Turin. The brand has the authority to say, 'You may wear other jeans, but you Live in Levi's.' There is no higher authority in denim than that.

The sustainable food retailer Daylesford Organic's authority comes from their responsible farming practices, animal husbandry and dedication to world-class standards for organic agriculture. They have the knowledge, wisdom and learned authority through their decades of innovation, pioneering and practice.

A globally iconic brand that I've also had the privilege of working with is Adidas. Their authority comes from the concept of 'the Corinthian spirit,' with the values associated with fair play, sportsmanship, participation and a strong sense of team. That's why they have many of the greatest sports teams on their books, including Real Madrid and Bayern Munich. The Olympics Games epitomise these values, which are front and centre every four years. Adidas wins at every Olympics because its core values are aligned with the notion of the participatory Olympian spirit. It's not just about winning.

A large proportion of influencer marketing and celebrity endorsement is about borrowing authority and creating credibility. It's positioning by proxy, helping brands supercharge their authority in the marketplace. But it's a delicate balance — if you overindulge in influencers, they start to define the brand, and you can become the sum of what the trendsetters say. So brands need a counterpoint of deep authority to go that route. It will always be a two-way street. Consumers wear brands that are a reflection of their own values, with the sum of this consumption helping define the brand. This relationship between brands and consumers has always been complex, with an intricate balance between influence and perception. People choose brands that align with their values and self-identification, while their collective choices shape the brand's identity.

In the realm of brand design, incongruent associations can arise. For instance, seeing a middle-aged individual sporting a youth-oriented brand like Volcom might create a disconnect that potentially harms the brand's image. This highlights the delicate balance brands must maintain between broadening their appeal and preserving their core identity.

Celebrity endorsements can complicate this landscape. Take, for example, David Beckham's association with Haig Club Whiskey or Conor McGregor's with Proper No. Twelve whisky. These partnerships leverage the cult of celebrity to boost brand awareness, but they also raise questions about authenticity and expertise.

While Beckham's fame undoubtedly drove awareness for Haig Club, his credibility as a whiskey connoisseur — as opposed to someone who likes the odd tipple, or one who's simply paid to pretend — is open to question. This disconnect between the celeb's perceived expertise and the product they're endorsing can breed scepticism among discerning consumers. The brand gains visibility but potentially at the cost of authenticity and respect within the category.

Moreover, the impact of these endorsements can vary widely depending on the consumer. For some, Beckham's association might elevate Haig Club to an aspirational status. For others, particularly whiskey enthusiasts, it could diminish the brand's credibility.

The challenge lies in balancing the immediate boost in awareness that celebrities provide with the long-term implications for brand perception and loyalty. While sales figures might justify these partnerships in the short term, they may not contribute to sustainable brand building.

Influencer marketing presents its own set of challenges. Unlike traditional celebrities, influencers often build their following based on perceived armchair expertise, relatability in specific niches or just plain coolness. But as their influence grows, so does the pressure to monetise their platform, sometimes leading to partnerships that feel inauthentic or misaligned with their personal brand.

While celebrity endorsements and influencer partnerships can drive significant awareness and sales, brands must carefully consider the long-term impact on their identity and credibility. The most successful collaborations will be those that maintain authenticity, align with the brand's core values and resonate genuinely with the target audience. As the landscape continues to evolve, brands will need to navigate these complexities thoughtfully if they want to build lasting connections with consumers.

POSITIONING — REASONS TO BELIEVE

The 'reason to believe' in brand positioning is a critical factor that influences a company's veracity and credibility. Two stories from iconic brands I have helped design deal with Innis and Gunn's unique brewing techniques, born from a 'happy accident,' and Burberry, with their pioneering spirit that transcends fashion to now include things like digital interfaces. Another brand reason to believe that intrigues me is MAC Cosmetics' unique scientific approach in the beauty industry.

The reason to believe is a crucial element in successful branding, serving as the foundation of a brand's credibility. It's not just about historical achievements but rather ongoing behaviour that demonstrates authenticity and expertise to consumers.

Consider Innis and Gunn, an Edinburgh craft brewer. Their reason to believe stems from a rich family history... and a fortuitous accident. The company were contracted to age beer in oak barrels, to impart ale flavour to bourbon whiskey that was to then be aged in them. After the barrels were so seasoned, the beer would be dumped. However, somebody discovered that the oak-aged beer was absolutely delicious. The resulting beer was refined and became 'The Original, by Innis and Gunn.'

The company's family history provides a rich narrative of bravery, recipes, wood, distilling and brewing. Heroic grandparents were actively involved in the Second World War; a grandfather secured a key bridge during the D-Day landings; he went on to become a renowned carpenter; he fathered a master distiller; the grandmother gained local fame creating amazing recipes in a time of rationing to feed the children of Edinburgh. This heritage culminates in the company founder's expertise as a master brewer, creating novel beer flavoured in oak barrels. This rich backstory and ongoing commitment to craftsmanship and innovation gives consumers a compelling reason to value and trust in the brand's quality and creativity.

Burberry provides another excellent example. Their reason to believe isn't just rooted in Thomas Burberry's invention of gabardine.[4] It's the company's continued association with pioneering spirit and innovation. The clothier outfitted polar explorers and aviators. George Mallory, who participated in the first three British expeditions to Mount Everest in the early 1920s, and was possibly the first to reach the summit before he died on the mountain, was wearing Burberry. It was the cloth worn by the first female aviators, as well as Shackleton and Scott on their Antarctic expeditions.

Burberry were along for some of the greatest adventures in Britain's national story, and their iconic checked patterns were ultimately incorporated into website designs, social media graphics, virtual product displays and interactive experiences. All this has reinforced their credibility as a brand that has been pushing boundaries for more than a century.

---

[4] Gabardine is a durable twill worsted wool. It is a tightly woven, waterproof fabric used to make outerwear and various other garments, such as suits, overcoats, trousers and uniforms.

MAC Cosmetics demonstrates a reason to believe through their scientific approach to matching skin tones. This ongoing commitment to inclusivity and precision in their products builds trust with consumers.

The key difference between authority and reason to believe lies in their temporal nature:
1. Authority is based on historical facts and past achievements.
2. Reason to believe is demonstrated through ongoing behaviour and current values and actions.

A strong reason to believe allows consumers to draw a direct line between a brand's claimed expertise and its current actions. It's not just about what a brand has done in the past but how it continues to live up to its promises and values in the present.

In successful branding, the reason to believe should be clear, consistent and continuously reinforced through the brand's actions, products, endorsements and communications. This creates a compelling narrative that resonates with consumers and builds long-term brand loyalty.

POSITIONING — PRODUCT ESSENCE & BRAND ESSENCE

Product essence is really the distilling of two questions: what is similar to other products, and what sets us apart? In doing this, you can define the compelling product advantage.

Look at Speedo — it's in the name. The product essence is aqua-dynamic swim clothing. As others do, the Australian company creates well-fitting swimwear. But the thing they did better than everybody else was to eliminate drag. Speedo's 'Fastskin' was created using the same characteristics as shark skin. The skin basically captures a film of water around the animal's body as it moves, which means that the shark is effectively moving water through water, not skin through water. This minimises drag, and Fastskin was able to replicate that. In doing so, Speedo created a fantastic product, the essence of which is no drag. While the competition is doing the same as Speedo in terms of aqua dynamics, Speedo is simply creating faster materials.

Inov-8 found its niche through grip. The whole of the running category tends to be based on cushioning technology, with Nike Air, Mizuno Wave, Asics Gel and Reebok DMX all delivering impact-cushioning designed to manage the ride. So does Inov-8, but with innovative grip technology, they could sell all-terrain confidence to the adventure-loving consumer. Inov-8 does cushioning as well as everybody else but maximises your control on any terrain better than anyone else. The clear product essence of Inov-8 was grip.

The magic that was created by the iPhone was in part due to Gorilla Glass. Now we take for granted what was initially quite remarkable — a wonderfully smooth, scratch-resistant glass surface that you could run your finger across, activating an array of digital features, creating the device's unique product essence. When everyone else was logical, the iPhone was magical.

Thinking about brand essence and applying the same questioning, what do brands do that is the same, and what do they do differently?

- For Speedo, the brand essence is speed, helping you glide through the water like nobody else can.
- Inov-8 gives you control like no other brand, meaning you are fearless.
- The iPhone — it provides a magical experience like no other phone brand.

This demonstrates why orientating positioning around clear product essences and clear brand essence is so important. It defines the fundamental differences as we start to develop products and craft communication around them. We live in a world that is overly indexed on the left brain, the seat of logical thinking and technological superiority, which speaks to product essence and not enough to brand essence. Too much rational and not enough emotional.

It is an advantage when you're new to the market and have product superiority. You only need to be present; you don't even have to persuade. But as the competition piles in after you, the danger lies in the other guy being either the same as or better than you, and you've failed to make clear your point of differentiation. Product parity is a dead-end street.[5]

To overcome instances of product parity, which can happen to every company, you need to establish emotional superiority. New brands, especially in the tech space, as they enter the marketplace and are experiencing the benefit of product superiority, should invest in emotional superiority. It was not an accident that Apple, experiencing the tidal wave of demand that came with the iMac desktop computer, invested in its *Think Different* campaign. We are still emotionally invested in Apple, which makes the statement that we are different, that we think differently. This created the emotional superiority that still reigns over Apple's competition.

---

[5] This is the dilemma of a product being similar to its competitor in terms of features, function and performance. For example, a parity product might have the same look and feel, deliver the same utility and solve the same problems as a competitor's. We see this in household cleaning products, toothpaste, forks, personal care items, etc. Parity products can be harmful to businesses because they can limit marketing and branding strategies, make it difficult to command premium pricing, make it hard to maintain competitive advantages, cause price wars and make it harder to attract and retain users. Yet this can be an advantage to consumers, keeping prices low and reducing the chances of monopolisation. Product parity gives consumers choice.

POSITIONING — POINTS OF PARITY & POINTS OF DIFFERENCE

As we've noted, when analysing brand positioning, it's important to examine two critical aspects:

1. Points of Parity (POP): Attributes or benefits that are essential to be considered a legitimate player in a product category. These are often shared with competitors.
2. Points of Difference (POD): Unique attributes or benefits that set a brand apart from the pack.

Understanding both POP and POD is crucial for effective brand building and positioning.

- POP establishes category membership and credibility.
- POD creates a compelling reason for consumers to choose one brand over another.

Key Insights:

1. People don't buy sameness; they seek differentiation.
2. POP helps identify sector hygiene factors.
3. POD defines a brand's compelling positional advantage.

For instance, Apple's and Microsoft's POP is personal computers. Microsoft represents the establishment in PC software, whereas Apple stands as the challenger to that establishment. Apple's POD can be distilled into 'challenger, innovation, design-focused.' Microsoft's is 'established, software dominance, business-oriented.' You can immediately see the emotional difference between the two.

When you look at Nike and Adidas, both have sportswear as a point of parity. Adidas is about team participation and community; Nike is about the individual and victory. The emotional difference emerges through the POD.

The interplay between POP and POD:

1. Identify shared attributes (POP) within the competitive set.
2. Use POP as a foundation to highlight unique brand values (POD).
3. Develop emotional differentiation based on POD.

This approach to brand positioning is essential for:
1. Understanding market dynamics.
2. Crafting unique brand identities.
3. Developing effective marketing strategies.
4. Guiding brand design and communication.

By leveraging both POP and POD, brands can establish their legitimacy within a category while clearly articulating their unique value proposition to consumers. This is hugely important when building a brand identity and design.

INOV-8

Photo Credit: Jim Yeomans

OUR NEW BRAND PROPOSITION, 'THE ALL TERRAIN RUNNING COMPANY,' FOCUSED ON THE CORE PRODUCT DIFFERENTIATOR, 'GRIP,' THAT IN TURN DELIVERS 'FEARLESSNESS' TO THE CONSUMER.

INOV-8

Photo Credit: Jim Yeomans

CONVENTIONAL BRAND DESIGN

2.3 BRAND DESIGN
DELIVERING PROFIT

BRAND PERSONALITY — INTRODUCTION

The role of a brand can be defined by understanding its emotional effect, or that which we would like it to adopt. It includes shaping the brand's character and our attraction and, ultimately, addiction to that character.

The first case study we'll look at to demonstrate brand personality and emotional effect delves into our work with Renault Trucks. My role was to move the brand positioning up one notch, from number five to number four. This was achieved through positioning and personality: personifying 'The Venerable Driver.'

We observed that truck drivers love their job but hate the fact that other road users hate them. They were also resentful that the high degree of independence and freedom associated with being a driver on the open road was being eradicated by increased monitoring, recording, checks and restrictions in an increasingly automated world. Even toilet breaks were being captured, timed and scrutinised. With almost everything we rely on having the handprint of a truck driver — from morning coffee, evening beer, medication and building equipment to home deliveries — they worked night and day to keep the world moving.

Focusing in on this, our approach was to challenge less flattering perceptions and inspire veneration of the truck driver. The emotional effect was established: seeking pride and recognition. While competitors focused on automation and monitoring, Renault recognised an untapped emotional opportunity in the trucking industry and chose to celebrate and honour truckers. This approach addressed a key emotional pain point we had identified: drivers felt unappreciated and constrained by increasing automation.

By positioning their brand as a champion of drivers, Renault created an emotional connection that translated into tangible business benefits:
1. Increased driver satisfaction and retention.
2. Proud vehicle care, leading to lower maintenance costs.
3. Enhanced brand loyalty.
4. Higher resale value of vehicles.

Getting your arms around the trucker, with the emotional narrative 'venerating the driver,' seamlessly connected with rational business outcomes, demonstrating how addressing emotional needs can drive profitability.

A similar effect was achieved with the whisky brand Nc'nean. Understanding the founder's principles, a woman challenged the conventions of a dated whisky establishment that was masculine and exclusive, alongside discovering a fitting historical connection. Annabel remembers, *"We chose Neachneohain as the Scottish equivalent of Artemis. We found her in the history books, and then shortened it to Nc'nean. She was known as the queen of spirits (in the elphine sense), and she was also known as a protector of nature and for walking her own path. This so perfectly fitted our mission that we adopted a shortening of her name as ours."*

Building the product personality around the purist brand role with elements from authentic botanicals, herbs and aromatics, we designed by moonlight with a sensitivity to mother nature. The Emotional Effect sought was Inclusivity and Pioneering Spirit, the Brand Personality: Challenger, Authentic, Nature-connected.

Nc'nean challenged whisky industry conventions by creating an inclusive, environmentally conscious brand. They tapped into the emotional desire for authenticity and connection to nature while also breaking gender and all stereotypes.

The key elements of our approach:
1. Leveraged historical narrative of a strong female mythical character.
2. Emphasised organic, biodiverse production methods.
3. Created packaging that reflected natural botanicals of the distilleries surroundings.

The result was a brand that resonated emotionally with a broader audience, particularly women, who had often felt excluded from traditional whisky culture. This emotional connection translated into numerous industry awards and strong market performance.

Meanwhile, Apple have moved from Challenger to Establishment. The emotional effect sought is inspiration and individuality, with the brand personality evolving from initial challenger to current visionary leader. Its journey illustrates how brand personality can evolve while maintaining a strong emotional core. Their *Think Different* campaign — a poke at long-established computer giant IBM's THINK slogan — epitomised their challenger status, appealing to consumers' desire to stand out and be innovative. As Apple grew, their emotional effect shifted from pure rebellion to inspiration and aspiration. They maintained their emotional connection with consumers by consistently delivering products that felt cutting-edge and exclusive.

Key takeaways:
1. Emotional effect as a starting point: Brands should consciously design for emotional impact, not treat it as a byproduct.
2. Balancing emotion and rationality: Successful brands connect emotional narratives with rational benefits, addressing both feeling and thinking.
3. Anthropomorphising brands: Putting human stories (like those of truck drivers or female distillers) at the centre of brand narratives creates powerful emotional connections.

4. Evolving Brand Personality: As demonstrated by Apple, a brand can evolve its personality while maintaining its core emotional appeal.
5. Untapped Emotional Opportunities: Look for emotional needs that competitors are overlooking, as Renault did in the trucking industry.

By consciously crafting their brand personality and emotional effect, companies can unlock significant value, driving customer loyalty, product preference and, ultimately, business success.

BRAND PERSONALITY — BRAND EFFECT

Brand effect, in simplest terms, is the impact a brand has on the consumer. The personality of the brand will ultimately shape the addictive relationship that a customer has with it. This is defined by marketing researchers Anjun Chaudhuri and Morris Holbrook (2001) as "a brand's potential to elicit a positive emotional response in the average consumer as a result of its use."[6] It is the consumers' emotional response as a result of experience, interaction or interface with the product or service. It is the ability of reputations to influence people's future behaviour.

An example of this can be seen in our work with Gore, maker of Gore-Tex, Gore Bikewear and Gore Runwear. One of their big brand values is trust, and trust is a huge emotional platform that comes with a huge paradox: as soon as you say 'trust me,' no one trusts you. So the role here is to effectuate, emotionalise and build trust. As a coveted human trait, trust is the key to unlocking deeper, more meaningful relationships. Research shows that trust is often what people are seeking when choosing brands. Improbably enough, they believe that trust in a brand (88%) is more important than trust in love (81%), perhaps because love, like relevance, is fleeting.

---

[6] Chaudhuri and Holbrook (2001) The Chain of Effects from Brand Trust and Brand Affect to Brand Performance: The role of Brand Loyalty, Journal of Marketing, volume 65, Issue 2.

Trust is more elemental — it is rational and emotional and a promise that you will be who and what you need us to be (now and in the future).[7]

Similarly, Volvo Defense wanted people to feel trust in relying on their mobile defence systems. They wanted to instil trust in their weaponry to such an extent that they could affect intuitive performance on the battlefield.

A brand like The North Face, in its adventurer brand role, creates the emotion of exhilaration for the consumer by stepping into the unknown, veering off the map, taking on the quest, facing down the trails. And this takes you to an adventurer role. With both Volvo and Gore-Tex, you want to create trust — the opposite of exhilaration. You want to move the consumer to a place of safety and security. When evoking exhilaration, you want to move them to a place of danger and excitement.

BRAND PERSONALITY — TIME

In the intricate dance between brands and consumers, time emerges as a powerful yet often overlooked medium. Brands don't seek to dominate every moment of a consumer's life, nor should they. Instead, the art lies in claiming specific, emotionally resonant time slots that align with the brand's essence.

There are lots of different versions or aspects of time. We can own the physical time, such as a day in the week, spiritual time, kaironic time (seeking the right opportunity, full of potential, such that it beckons us to participate in special moments), experiential time (relating to or resulting from experience), or repeated time.

Working with the outdoor brand Karrimor, I identified the time we wanted to own as Monday mornings, when people dreaded leaving the outdoors to go back to their jobs. We then designed the brand communication that only went out on a Monday morning ('Phone in sick.') This time slot owned the Monday morning blues, with the emotional connection of outdoor escapism vs work drudgery, leveraging the brand personality of rebellion, nature loving and empathetic.

Sebago, one of the first loafer brands designed in the US state of Maine, was created when a man skippering his boat could see he was slipping across the deck, while his dog was not. After examining the pads of the dog's foot, he incised a similar siping into the soles of his shoes.[8] This created the deck shoe, which Sebago imbued with the idea of quality hand-craftsmanship. This teaches us that time spent in the making of products isn't measured, it's experienced. It is not time saved, but time invested, that matters. This is representative of kaironic time, not chronomatic time. Creating handcrafted products carries great value: craftsmanship as timeless art. Here, the emotional connection is appreciation for meticulous creation, unparalleled quality, reliability and style.

Monos, a premium luggage brand offering classics with aesthetics that stand the test of time, was designed around kaironic time — it's the experience of the journey that's important, not the destination. The focus is the quality of experience over quantitative measurement, demonstrating the brand personality of adventurous, introspective and value-centred.

Conversely, with brands such as Australian workout gear maker 2XU, at the forefront of advancing performance compression technology, it's all about chronomatic time — improving your performance within measured time. In a different world, Patek Philippe looks beyond the present. The luxury watchmaker is about legacy and generational value, making the emotional connection between timeless prestige and family heritage, and has a brand personality of sophistication, enduring and aspirational.

While profit-driven strategies might push for omnipresence in a consumer's life, true brand resonance comes from disciplined

---

[7] 2021 Edelman Trust Barometer Special Report: Trust, The New Brand Equity.
[8] Siping – cutting thin slots into material such as rubber or leather.

focus. Even seemingly mundane products, like toilet paper, eschew direct association with their use-time, opting instead for adjacent positive emotions. This can take the form of playful moments with pets, where a cute labrador is connected to a toilet roll.

Being strategic with time ownership requires a disciplined approach, with careful consideration paid to:
1. Identifying emotionally charged moments aligned with brand values.
2. Creating content and experiences that enhance these specific time slots.
3. Resisting the urge to overextend, maintaining brand integrity and focus.
4. Cultivating depth in chosen temporal territories rather than breadth across all time.

In the end, a brand's relationship with time is not about quantity, but quality. By selectively owning moments that matter most to their core identity and consumer connection, brands can weave themselves into the fabric of life without overwhelming it, creating lasting impressions in the hearts and minds of their audience.

BRAND PERSONALITY — PLACE

The geography of a brand's origin impacts its personality and identity. The essence of place is intricately woven into brand ethos, helping define the brand's character. The rebellious spirit of Waterloo London and the serene tranquillity reflected in Arc'teryx's Canadian roots are two case studies that demonstrate how geography can shape a brand, define its trajectory and contribute to its identity.

When designing the branding for Waterloo London, a new retail, restaurant and leisure space next to the iconic Waterloo Station, we looked at its place. Situated across the Thames from the Houses of Parliament and Whitehall, it sits just outside the establishment. The fact that commuters come to and from Waterloo every day, because they live outside of London, added to this. It's a place outside the establishment for people who are outsiders to London. It is a challenger, it's a rebel. A wonderful place that doesn't have codes of distinction, like the establishment. A place of communities rather than greed; one of chaotic creativity as opposed to order. It is a really playful place to be. Just the physical geographic space of Waterloo, the South Bank, creates an amazing distinction within the brand of London. Inspired by the meaning of place and community — 'A place made by Outsiders' — the Waterloo London brand was positioned as the rebel outlier, juxtaposed against the staid Westminster establishment and West End order.

With Arc'teryx, we had to create a distinction between them and their nearest competitor, The North Face. We considered where The North Face is from: America, the totemic edifice of Western civilisation. Western society has been at war, if you include Europe in 'the West,' for about 5,000 years, with the odd outbreak of peace. That's five millennia of colliding races, civilisations, classes, religions and nations. This has created a relentlessly competitive psychosis within our culture and in our relationship with both sport and the outdoors. Even The Book of Genesis opens with talk of "man's dominion over nature" — a Biblical assertion of our ownership of and control over the natural world.

Our relationship with sport is defined by winning or losing, a competitive tussle that The North Face, as a distinctly Western-based brand, embraces. It's a conquering relationship with the outdoors. Not so for Arc'teryx. Being from Canada, which touches the Arctic Circle, it shares a northern aspect of civilisation with the Urals and with Scandinavia. It's a civilisation that's shamanic, in that it lives in balance with nature, and nomadic, leaving no trace. This allowed us to create a brand that isn't of ego, living as one with nature versus striving to conquer nature. By building a meaning system based on place, we created a point of difference from the competition. It expresses itself in the subtlety of the company's logo — a minimalist fossil skeleton of the archaeopteryx, the evolutionary transition species between dinosaurs and modern birds. This image often appears very small, almost indistinguishable on the fabric. And it worked, positioning Arc'teryx as a globally iconic player.

In many cases, the country's image lends credibility to brand image. Leica pivots off German engineering, and Omega evokes Swiss precision. Likewise, think French wine, Danish design, Thai hospitality, Italian fashion, German cars or Japanese electronics. Research has shown that the country of origin effect can in itself be the reason for the success or failure of a certain product sold at a certain price point due to the associations it conjures in consumers' minds.[9] Sense of place defines many of the brands we love.

BRAND PERSONALITY — RITUAL

As with time and place, a brand can also own some of the rituals in our lives. Guinness is a great example, with its evocation of the ritual of patience. How the stout is poured is not just a simple step, it's an art, a studied procedure, an integral part of the experience, requiring patience, practice and reverence for tradition. If a brand understands the unique role of ritual in our lives, it can connect on a much deeper, almost spiritual level. If the specific ritual can be aligned to a specific time and a specific place, then it is on the road to creating consumer addiction.

The bathroom products company Nuie's brand is designed to own the rituals of transformation. This is the transformative shift that happens in that special tiled space as we ritualise the transition from home to work (morning shower) and from work to home (evening bath).

The 2XU sports brand is designed to own the ritual of preparation before the competition. Get this right, and the consumer will feel through ritual that they win before they compete.

Ritual is an important component because it's the interface between human behaviour and brand behaviour. Brand rituals are specific, repeated behaviours or practices associated with a brand that help create a deeper connection between the consumer and the product or company.

With Dainese, a brand known for producing safety gear for physically risky sports like motorcycling, mountain biking and horseback riding, the ritual of protection gives the consumer the freedom to take a leap of faith. The ritual of protection here refers to the act of donning the equipment before engaging in these rough-and-tumble activities, providing people with the freedom to go for it. This 'cloaking' ritual gives them the confidence to take risks they might otherwise avoid. By putting on Dainese gear, users perform a symbolic act of preparation that mentally and physically readies them for the adventure ahead. This ritual reinforces the brand's association with safety, enabling customers to push their limits.

For Ivy League-inspired British clothier Ben Sherman, who became particularly popular in mod and ska subcultures, it was the ritual of buttoning up that unleashed the self-expression of considered, self-reverential behaviour. It's not just about getting dressed but consciously choosing to present oneself in a particular way.[10, 11] This ritual emphasises the brand's association with considered, deliberate style choices that appeal to consumers who view their clothing as an extension of their personality and values.

---

[9] Martin Roll, Business and Brand Leadership, Country branding strategies for nations and companies, Dec 2018.

[10] The mods (from 'modernist') were a youth movement that began in 1950s London, influencing fashion, rock music and other urban trends. The subculture dressed smartly, with a touch of androgyny, as a rebellion against the conservatism, austerity and mundane routines of their working-class parents' post-war generation.

[11] An upbeat precursor to rocksteady and reggae, ska is a musical style that originated in Jamaica in the late 1950s and took root in Great Britain in the mid-60s. Subsequent ska revivals hit the charts, cross-fertilising with punk rock, in the 1970s, '80s and '90s.

And with Guinness, as we've noted, the ritual of waiting for the head to settle on your carefully pulled pint held promise that good things come to those who wait. This has allowed Guinness to own the concept of patience in the beer market, differentiating it from the slapdash pour and down-the-hatch of its competitors.

In each of these cases, ritual serves as a powerful interface between the brand and the consumer. It's not just about using a product; it's about participating in a meaningful experience that reinforces the brand's core values and differentiators. These rituals create a deeper emotional connection with the brand, encourage loyalty and help cement its position in the consumer's mind. By cultivating these rituals, companies can carve out a unique space in their market and in consumers' lives, turning ordinary interactions with products into moments of significance that reinforce brand identity and values.

BRAND PERSONALITY — BRAND VALUES

For brand design to stand the test of time, you need to build strong relationships, which calls for strong brand values. These distinguish you from the competition and help you rise above the rest, encouraging customer loyalty and retention. Our value systems are fundamentally innate. The human propensity to subconsciously gather attributes and build reputations means brand success can lie in the precise balance between creating rational values and emotional ones. Appealing to the head or the heart and understanding the logic in the underlying psychology, branding values work because they can slot into our individual belief systems. The rational values are important with regard to brand personality — they are reflective of what a brand does. They communicate much about the product, make people think and shape consumer need and addiction.

Our value systems affect the brands that we notice and can readily change based on our current mood or physical state.

If a brand offers something you value, you notice its messages. If it has proven its value or demonstrated its alignment with your personal values, you notice its message. For example, people who value an active lifestyle are far more likely to interact with Nike, Adidas, Lululemon, Fabletics or 2XU. People who value environmental action are drawn to brands like Patagonia, Method and Arc'teryx. People who have had continuous positive experiences with Apple disregard the messaging from other phone or computer manufacturers.

The power of rational values and how they contribute to brand personality can be demonstrated through Dr. Martens' industrial durability, which shouts 'different.' That is why they're distinct from boots like Ugg and Sorel — there's this industrial masculinity that makes them appealing to women as well as men. We see rational values come through in the Team Sky cycling organisation's relentless incremental gains. Marks and Spencer demonstrate their rational values, especially in food, around trust — an important generator of difference. In each of these instances, values shape consumer thought patterns and drive addictive need.

Beyond these nuts and bolts rational considerations, emotional values move us more into the branding space. It is the emotional values that make consumers feel and connect, leading to the want and shaping addiction and longer-term loyalty.

Working with the Scout movement demonstrated this as we identified the emotional values of the organisation, juxtaposing a strong adjective with an evocative noun: 'relentless kindness.' This became the key emotive brand construct for them. Similarly, working with Bear Grylls OBE, the British adventurer, writer, television presenter and former SAS trooper, we identified three emotive values to associate with him as we positioned him as the guide archetype: equip, educate and empower.

Another brand that elicits strong emotional values that help differentiate is Dove, which speaks to body positivity and inclusivity in all its forms. Again, the common theme is generating feelings in the consumer that drive addiction to the brand.

BRAND PERSONALITY — CHARISMA AND CONVICTION

In the realm of building appealing personality, charisma and conviction play fundamental roles in creating an addictive connection between consumers and brands. These elements, when skilfully integrated into a brand's ethos, can lead to a powerful and lasting customer-brand relationship.

Conviction refers to what a brand fundamentally stands for — its core values and beliefs. This conviction gives a brand depth and texture, shaping its identity and guiding its actions. For instance, working with Converse and Levi's revealed a conviction of authentic self-expression running through each. Converse positions its Chuck Taylor shoes as a blank canvas for self-expression, while Levi's promotes the idea that you can be your most authentic self when wearing their products.

As the Roman orator Cicero noted, *"Nothing convinces like conviction."* This principle holds true even when applied to branding strategies. However, as somebody or another once remarked, "Nothing convinces like conviction, even if you're wrong." There's incalculable value in ensuring that a brand's convictions are authentic, ethical and aligned with its actions.

Charisma, on the other hand, is about how a brand stands up and stands out. It's not just what a brand believes in but also what it opposes. New Balance exemplify this by positioning themselves as an anti-fashion brand. They don't live by trends, and their product is based on practicality. This was a shoe they are never going to pay a celebrity to wear. By positioning it as anti-fashion, we addressed the negative aspects of fashion, giving New Balance a distinct outsider charisma.

Similarly, the automotive brand Mini has built its charisma by standing against the boring and mundane, instead championing joyfulness and excitement. Mountain Equipment, positioned as a 'rebel craftsman,' builds its charisma around The Alpinist Way, standing for simplicity and efficiency in peak-scaling challenges.

The interplay between charisma and conviction creates a potent mix that can forge powerful, almost addictive connections with consumers. People are naturally drawn to brands that take strong stances and have clear positions. For established brands with decades of market presence, being authoritative and convincing comes more naturally, having earnt the right. However, it's crucial to balance this with a degree of humility, especially for newer companies just entering the market. They must focus on actions rather than words. They shape their conviction and charisma through their production processes and how they bring products to market. As they grow and become known for these actions, they can then articulate and celebrate their personality in their communications. At its simplest, actions determine what you stand for, which can then be communicated.

The key is to design both charisma and conviction into a brand and its products. This design process starts with identifying the brand's core beliefs and the principles it stands against. By bringing these two elements together, you can create a compelling narrative that resonates with consumers on a deeper level.

In essence, the strategic use of charisma and conviction in branding goes beyond mere marketing tactics. It's about creating a brand identity that stands for something meaningful, opposes what it doesn't believe in and connects with consumers on an emotional level. When done right, this approach can lead to long-lasting brand loyalty and a distinctive place in the market, as demonstrated by the success of brands like Converse, Levi's, New Balance, Mini and Mountain Equipment.

THE BRAND NEW FUTURE

MONOS

Photo Credit: The Rig Out

MONOS WAS DESIGNED AROUND KAIRONIC TIME —
IT'S THE EXPERIENCE OF THE JOURNEY THAT'S
IMPORTANT, NOT THE DESTINATION.

MONOS

Photo Credit: The Rig Out

CONVENTIONAL BRAND DESIGN

THE BRAND NEW FUTURE

WATERLOO.LONDON

Photo Credit: Jim Yeomans

CONVENTIONAL BRAND DESIGN

INSPIRED BY THE MEANING OF PLACE AND COMMUNITY — 'A PLACE MADE BY OUTSIDERS.'

THE BRAND NEW FUTURE

WATERLOO.LONDON

Photo Credit: Jim Yeomans

CONVENTIONAL BRAND DESIGN

BRAND PURPOSE — INTRODUCTION

Brand purpose is a company's reason for existence, beyond its business goals and objectives. It's the 'why' behind the operation and is usually related to the customers it serves and the market space it wants to fill. As brands strive for differentiation, relevance, market share and growth, a clear purpose brought to life in compelling ways often spells the difference between success and failure. Brand purpose goes beyond existing to make a profit and really sets out to answer the bigger questions of 'why?' It is the core purpose, cause or belief, setting out the very reason your company exists. The trajectory of a brand depends on its purpose — defining and shaping its culture and spirit. Having a clear and compelling brand purpose is important to drive growth; purpose-driven companies and brands outperform their competitors on multiple levels.

In his book, *Grow*, Jim Stengel, former Chief Marketing Officer of Procter & Gamble, the world's largest consumer goods company, delved into the results of a 10-year study of 50,000 brands. It found that those centred around improving people's lives beat their category competitors by significant margins.[12] The highest performing businesses are those driven by brand purpose or principles, which usually grow faster than the competition.

BRAND PURPOSE — LENS

The brand lens defines a company's ability to really understand its sector and its role within that space.

We recently looked at an early entrant to the gardening clothing category. As one of the original and only brands in the sector, it was catering to everything in gardening and mistakenly identifying its sector in its entirety as its brand. This left it vulnerable to someone then coming in behind it with a more precise and focused vision.

---

[12] Brand Purpose 101: Everything you wanted to know but were afraid to ask. Afdhel Aziz, 2017. Source: medium.com

As mentioned earlier, sometimes narrowing the focus broadens the appeal and becomes more critical as competition develops. Consider Nike's lens — victory — which enables them to inhabit the world of sport. The company's namesake, Nike, was the mythological Greek goddess of victory, which says it all. If Nike, the world's most valuable apparel brand, started to talk about the importance of merely taking part, you'd instantly feel like something was off in their brand communications. That they'd drifted from their purpose. Nike isn't sportswear, it is the victory in sportswear.

A company must understand the brand lens and stay within the focus it brings. Rapha isn't cycling, it is the 'pain' within cycling. Inov-8 isn't running, it is the 'fearlessness' within running.

BRAND PURPOSE — MISSION

If purpose is the 'why' you exist, Mission is the what you need to do to get there. It is the action required every day to achieve the vision, and it captures the specific initiatives or tactics needed to build the required company culture. More than just a statement, a well-crafted mission has the power to emotionalise the culture within a brand, inspiring employees and shaping the company's direction. This emotional connection to the mission can transform ordinary tasks into meaningful contributions towards a greater purpose.

Odlo is a Swiss-based brand with Norwegian heritage that specialises in apparel base layers for outdoor mountain sports. When positioning Odlo as a craftsman brand, the challenge was to create a culture that embodied this archetype. The solution came in the form of a simple yet powerful mission: 'Every day, create a masterpiece.' This mission statement encouraged every employee to approach each day as an opportunity to excel in their craft, effectively driving a culture of craftsmanship throughout the organisation.

Arc'teryx began with a remarkably focused mission: to 'kill the Patagonia jacket.' This straightforward objective, set by founder Jeremy Guard, aimed to surpass the market-leading product of their competitor. Through relentless pursuit of this goal, Arc'teryx not only succeeded in creating superior products but also built a billion-dollar apparel company. Interestingly, this competitive drive benefited the entire industry, as it fostered a culture of innovation among all players. At Arc'teryx, they realised that innovation wasn't just an objective but a fundamental behaviour inspired by their mission.

Arguably the most famous illustration of a powerful mission comes from outside the business world. President John F Kennedy's bold challenge to the American people, to *"put a man on the moon by the end of the decade, not because it's easy but because it is hard,"* serves as a prime example of how a clear, ambitious mission can unite diverse groups towards a common goal. This mission statement galvanised academic institutions, commercial enterprises and government agencies, channelling their collective expertise into achieving what seemed impossible.

The impact of Kennedy's declaration was so profound that it permeated every level of the NASA space agency. As the story goes, when Kennedy later visited the NASA Space Center in Florida, he encountered a janitor sweeping the floor. When asked about his role, the man replied, *"Mr President, I'm here to put a man on the moon."* This anecdote perfectly captures how a well-crafted mission can align everyone in an organisation, regardless of their position, towards a shared purpose.

When developing a mission, it's crucial to remember that its primary function is to foster buy-in and create a contagious sense of purpose across the team. This internal passion naturally radiates outward, influencing external perceptions and actions. In the context of organisational missions, this translates to finding a truth — a 'why' that all team members can believe in and rally behind.

Ultimately, a strong mission provides employees with a compelling reason for their efforts, especially when faced with challenging tasks or long working hours. It's this raison d'être that emotionalises the workforce, inspiring them to strive for greatness and turning everyday actions into steps towards achieving something truly remarkable.

BRAND PURPOSE — VISION

Vision states 'where' you want to get to, the destination you want the brand or business to have arrived at in the future.

Vision is the emotionalisation of ambition. Looking at these three areas on a macro basis, you've got a mission that emotionalises culture, vision that emotionalises ambition and purpose that emotionalises strategy.

They are all important, but a very clever man, business advisor Andy Towne, once said to me, *"Culture eats strategy for breakfast."* Getting the mission right is what will drive everything. The vision is what will emotionalise ambition, and that is the desired end-state — the future vision of the brand. This is powerful stuff. If you can define the end state of the brand, you can then ask two very simple questions: 'What needs to come true for that to happen?' and 'What can be true?' The difference between the two then becomes a gap, which tells you where you might have resource deficiencies, where you might have to buy in expertise and what milestones you might need to achieve to get to the end state. Defining the vision is extraordinarily important because it emotionalises your ambition. It also emotionalises the trajectory and the speed of change.

Applying this to a brand I've loved working on is Daylesford Organic, who have a very powerful vision: to become the world's organic benchmark, the definitive standard. It's a beautiful vision because it is not about being the biggest but about being the most influential, and that really sets the tone for the ambition of the company's people. The ambition driving the business processes and the products is to be the best it can possibly be, to set a new bar for what it means to be organic.

We work with a brand in California whose vision is to transform maternity care in the US. America is probably the worst of the developed nations for maternal health outcomes, with dramatically greater risk associated with childbirth if your ethnicity is not white. Millie, as a brand, set itself the ambitious vision of transforming the field, working every day to provide better obstetric care for all through a modern, holistic approach to pregnancy care for people from every background. This incredible vision galvanises the ambition of the people inside the business, as well as those like me who work for the business. We also know that purpose and vision are crucial to attracting the best talent. Increasingly, people want to work for organisations whose values align with their own, where their contributions will be recognised and where there is a deeper reason for being, beyond profit margins.

An example of a very simple vision, one that I really respect and think of as brand poetry, is the tech company Cisco Systems.[13] Their vision is to 'network networks,' and that's genius. It's all in two words, the perfect economy of language.

How do we balance ambition and realism when it comes to setting vision? How high should we aim? The answer is the realistic ability to build a bridge between what needs to be true and what is true. So if the distance between what needs to be true and what is true is too great, and it can't be bridged by training of existing talent, external hiring or investment, you need to adjust. The gap between your ambition and what's realistically possible has to be effectively bridged.

Sometimes, aspirations should be slightly on the outer edge of realistic. I'm a great believer in our reach being further than our grasp. It is one of the opportunities that developments such as Web 3.0 offer: creating in a virtual world beyond the brand's physical grasp, opening new space and ambition to move towards.[14]

In some cases, we might see that a brand's ambition looks physically unrealistic, but it's conceivably possible, setting a trajectory that extends beyond what seems currently achievable. You're reaching for the virtual stars and hitting the physical moon.

BRAND PURPOSE — MORAL PURPOSE

Many brands have realised that their moral purpose is just as important as their market purpose and their responsibility to shareholders. It is an integral part of what they do and stand for; they're living by the values they promote. They have to walk the talk, putting words into action, and acting with moral purpose, in an authentic way. Modern brands are aiming to resonate with consumers on a deeper, ethical level, navigating this shift in consumer values against the backdrop of a changing world, marked by crises such as climate change, pandemics, economic downturns and political upheaval.

It is important to understand some of the drivers behind the consumer groups:
- Gen X (born between 1965 and 1980) is very much driven by the accumulation of things and the status that comes with that.
- For Gen Y (born between 1980and 1996), it is about the accumulation of experiences and the value that comes with that.
- Gen Z (born between 1997 and 2012) lives for the accumulation of content and the identity that comes with that.

The shift of Gen Y and Gen Z towards the more spiritual and

---

[13] "Cisco specialises in specific tech markets, such as The Internet of Things (IoT), domain security, videoconferencing and energy management. It is best known as a network hardware developer of telecom equipment that supports the internet. Source: Wikipedia

[14] Web 3.0, or Web3, is the third generation of the world wide web. It aims to create a decentralised and open online ecosystem. Source: Wikipedia

less material — combined with the accelerating impact of recent predicaments like COVID-19, the credit crunch, skyrocketing cost-of-living and the impact of climate change — brings a different slant to the values of the younger consumer, one where he or she wants to feel valued and sense that they're part of something. They want a brand to make them feel simultaneously individual and communal.

This has fuelled a shift in brand focus. Brands need to adapt to the changing values landscape and think as much about their own values as the value they create, considering moral purpose alongside market purpose. They should be thinking about communal gain as much as commercial gain so they can future-proof for the shifts towards a more responsible, sustainable future.

Through this context, we can view purpose in a different way, taking the standard vision and identifying the moral purpose within that ideal.

I have an American client that cultivates meat from blood plasma. It's a bold innovator, and its moral purpose is centred on the fact that humanity contrives to kill 1.5 billion cows a year, which is a whole lot of slaughter. Much of that meat is wasted, and most of it is unaffordable for those who need it most. Their solution is to bioengineer a lab-cultivated meat, and the whole idea — the moral purpose — is meat without the death.

The moral purpose is resetting the terms of our relationship with animals, that food is how we see ourselves reflected in each other, and creating a food source that is affordable to those who can't afford it in its traditional form.

On the other side of the US, in California, a client called Higher

---

[15] Developed in Italy in the early 1900s, the Montessori educational philosophy stems from a deep regard for children, emphasising hands-on, self-directed activity. Based on five principles derived from the experience of a doctor and educator, the approach involves respecting the uniqueness of every child, their freedom to choose, to move, to correct their own mistakes and to work at their own pace. Source: Wikipedia

Ground is very much driven by Montessori principles, seeing education as a lifelong process, from infancy through to old age.[15] They've built a digital platform that allows everybody, everywhere, to access global education as they move through the stages of maturing in life. Their moral purpose is to give people universal agency.

Patagonia has a clear moral purpose: To live in balance with nature. As noted earlier, they've placed their company into a trust, with Earth as their only 'shareholder.' It's a clever, emotive and compelling narrative centred on their moral purpose.

Much of what we see in the market now is what could be termed 'virtue signalling' or 'greenwashing' — disingenuous 'righteousness' ploys. Consumers are incredibly sensitive and savvy to this, detecting when brands are borrowing purpose as opposed to it genuinely emanating from within.

We have all experienced spurious claims from big banks telling us how much they care about the planet and your children, when we know it's not true. It rings hollow. If a higher moral purpose doesn't authentically resonate — it just doesn't credibly emanate from a brand — it's better for them not to even talk about it at all rather than trying to be something they're not. This is seen a lot in the private equity world, where there is much noise around environmental, social and governance (ESG) consciousness. On closer inspection, we tend to see harvesting of good news stories within a portfolio, which are then curated to look like the fruits of a pre-considered ESG policy. This is frustrating because ESG accomplishments should be the outcome of their investment strategy. They should result from the moral purpose and market purpose. It shouldn't be retrospectively fitted.

Humans by nature are drawn to the truth. Truth is a guiding North Star for us. It's as powerful as gravity. Any brand building a moral purpose, whether a bank, outdoor sports brand, fashion accessory or automobile, should apply the simple test of assessing what it is they're actually doing. We define and judge a person, and a brand, not on what they say but by what they do. We define them by their actions. If they're going to communicate with a strong sense of moral purpose, they need to make sure that their actions support any statements they make, and the sequencing should be to act first and speak later.

BRAND PURPOSE — COMMUNAL GAIN

In the latter part of the 20th century, the business world was largely driven by individual gain. But as we've alluded to, moving into the 21st century, there's been a significant shift towards considering the impact of businesses on communities. That's given rise to the concept of communal gain, which bridges the gap between commercial imperatives and broader societal impacts. And this informs a new era of consumer-driven change.

The modern business landscape demands a delicate balance. On one hand, companies must ensure their economic viability — the lights have to stay on. On the other hand, they must consider the wider implications of their actions. This dual focus on commercial and communal gain is reshaping how brands interact with their communities and how they define their purpose.

Take the line of outdoor adventure gear Adidas Terrex, for example. Adidas has a long-standing heritage in outdoor sports, sponsoring the Olympics and other winter competitions and activities. However, they hadn't fully capitalised on this franchise until recently. When tasked with creating a brand vision for Adidas Terrex, we recognised an opportunity to address a significant disparity. Only 1% of visitors to America's National Park System, which includes 63 uniquely spectacular parks, 11 battlefields and numerous other monuments and historical sites, were from the Black, Asian and minority ethnic (BAME) community. This is despite the fact that 48% of the country's population is composed of these racial-ethnic demographics. Since Adidas enjoys a strong following among urban and ethnic audiences, this gap led to a powerful communal purpose for Terrex: to provide access to the outdoors for everybody. The brand recognised that the well-being and positive effects of enjoying nature should be accessible to all, not just a predominantly white, Anglo-Saxon subset. By focusing on this notion of communal gain, Adidas Terrex not only expanded its market but also contributed to addressing a glaring social inequity.

Another prime example of a brand embracing communal purpose is Tesla. Their mission to eliminate the internal combustion engine goes beyond mere product innovation. It speaks to a larger goal of creating sustainable transport for life on Earth. More recently, it has expanded that focus to include sustainable energy, effectively shifting from an automotive focus to a broader clean-energy ecosystem agenda. This approach demonstrates how a strong moral dimension in business can also be good business practice.

These examples highlight a crucial shift in the dynamics between brands and consumers. For the first time in many marketers' careers, consumers — particularly Gen Z, those currently aged 11–27 — are ahead of brands in terms of values, attitudes and habits. Brands are now in a race to catch up with customer expectations, especially when it comes to social and environmental responsibility.

This shift in power dynamics is partly due to the increased awareness of global crises, such as climate change and the COVID-19 pandemic. People often feel powerless in the face of these challenges, unable to directly influence the decisions of world leaders. As consumers, though, they actually wield significant power through their purchasing decisions. The customer now has the ability to buy the change they want to see. By selecting brands with strong moral and communal purposes, the public can shape not only the brands themselves but also the impact these brands have on the world. This consumer-driven change is forcing brands to reevaluate their purposes and align more closely with the notion of communal gain.

In essence, we're entering an era where brands must realise that Gen Z and like-minded consumers will vote with their wallets for the future they want to see. They'll buy the brands that represent the future they want to live in. This means that a strong moral dimension is no longer just nice to have; it's becoming essential for business survival and success.

As we move forward, the most successful brands will be those that can effectively balance commercial imperatives with communal gain. They'll be the ones that not only meet consumer needs but also address broader societal and environmental challenges. In doing so, they'll secure their own success while contributing to positive change on a global scale.

They will also probably all have moments of clarity.

"IT IS THE IMPERFECTIONS THAT ARE REVEALED THAT GENERATE THE GROWING LOVE AND AFFECTION FOR THE PRODUCT AND THE BRAND."

MOMENTS OF CLARITY

ABDICATION

While working with Dr. Martens, I had a tricky meeting with the company's creatives and designers.

It's occurred to me that the reason the brand was famous was not because of anything anyone in that room had done.

In fact, it was attributable what people had done while wearing the boot.

I put the classic black, eight-eyelet 1460 model on the table and said, *"This boot is meaningless. It has no inherent meaning until somebody wears it."*

I let the shocked silence hang in the air for a moment before explaining my thinking.

"If a policeman wears it, it means order, if a criminal wears it, it means disorder, if a G20 protester wears it, it means chaos. If a nurse wears it, it means care, if a skinhead wears it, it means right wing, if a stop-oil protester wears it, it means left wing. It has no meaning until somebody wears it. Which means all we have to do at Dr. Martens is create great boots and present them as a blank canvas for self-expression."

This struck a chord, and from then on, Dr. Martens didn't impose their values on the consumer. As Nike had done, they allowed customers to express themselves, to telegraph their infinitely varied individuality through the product.

ELEGANT DECAY

While on the project to redesign Levi's, I was in a meeting with the global leadership team. I talked to them about the fact that they were the world leaders in the designing of elegant decay.

What I meant by that was that Levi's is one of those products where the more you wear them, the better they get. As they become increasingly aged, the fabric weathers and the patina deepens, revealing the character of the wearer. This logically set up the campaign we highlighted earlier: while you might wear other jeans, you actually Live in Levi's.

It is the imperfections that are revealed that generate the growing love and affection for the product and the brand.

IMPERFECTION

It was while working with the cycling organisation Team Sky that I was able to use a tennis analogy to help them see that we may respect perfection, but we actually fall in love with imperfection.

Take Novak Djokovic, the top-ranked tennis pro, when he wins his umpteenth Grand Slam. He looks into the crowd, and you can see in his eyes that he's wondering why he's respected but not loved. The reason, I think, is that he's a metronome of physical perfection.

However, when John McEnroe came onto the court, with fewer Grand Slams to his name, we fell in love with him because we could see his imperfections. And in his frailties and in his vulnerability, we saw a reflection of our own frailties and vulnerability.

That's why it's important for sports stars and teams to not always present themselves as invincible, which commands respect, but sometimes to present themselves as vulnerable, which inspires love.

3. BRAND ROLES

This chapter will look at 16 different brand roles. These are roles that, thanks to their appearance throughout human history—in stories, art, mythology and religion—are universal. They have evolved to characterise specific but common patterns of meaning that human beings can instinctively and subconsciously understand.

These brand roles fill a gap in our character, portraying an image to others about ourselves, sharing a message with everyone we meet without having a conversation. A brand role is a shared meaning system between what we wear (and eat, drink, drive, pay for membership in) and who we want the world to think we are. The 16 brand roles we'll examine each define and embody that gap, that messaging system, in a distinct way.

3.1 REBEL

If you want the emotional effect that your products have on a consumer to be inspirational, then you would choose the Rebel Brand role. A rebel is outside the establishment, bumping up against it and fighting to change it, and that's what is inspiring.

The place of this persona is the place of progress. The ritual of the brand role is the 'ritual of defiance,' and the time of the brand is the 'time of change.' If you are a Rebel Brand, you have three key rational values: Uncompromising, free thinking and principled.

These rational values are then supported by the emotional values of being independent, idealistic and optimistic. Your charisma and your conviction would come from the fact that you stand for justice and you stand against inequality, unfairness and injustice.

The reason we know the Rebel is so important is that we see it in history and film culture. We see it in William Wallace in *Braveheart*, John Keating in *Dead Poets Society* and Andy Dufresne in *The Shawshank Redemption*. It is Erin Brockovich, the legal secretary who works tirelessly to gain justice for a small town destroyed by a utility company's pollution. She is strong, tough, stubborn — a modern-day David who loves a good brawl with the corporate goliaths. She thrives on giving a voice to those who can't yell — a fighter and a hero. It's also Jyn Erso in *Rogue One: A Star Wars Story*. In all these films, we experience narratives of defiance, change, difference, legality, of being on the outside of the establishment, and of sacrifice.

Let's look at how that plays into brands.

It exists everywhere in the branding world, such as in Apple's *Think Different* campaign and its 1984 spot. It's PayPal, overturning the way we pay, and Vice, recasting the way we receive our news.

In the same way that classic rebels across our history have compelling stories, the rebels in these brands cultivate narratives. They share storylines of defiance, of agitating for change, of being different, of taking from the many and giving to the few, of being on the outside and being unafraid. They're unafraid of the sacrifices that change demands.

Doing what I do for a living, the Rebel Brand is fantastic to work with in terms of its code. It is creatively enriching and inspirational to both design for and bask in the glow of.

It is an incredibly seductive brand role, and it's easy to see why so many designers want to work with a company that adopts this stance. However, if everyone is a rebel and ready to stick it to the man, then nobody is.

We need to consider the most important component of the Rebel Brand narrative to really determine its character. Apple can be likened to Alexander the Great, who was undefeated in battle and considered one of the most successful military commanders of the ancient world. Apple under Steve Jobs was undeniably a rebel, and like Alexander, Apple pressed forward and conquered different territories. Following Alexander's death, his generals only knew one thing: maraud and conquer. They didn't know how to stay still and protect the palace, as they had always been on the outside, vanquishing other territories. In Alexander's absence, civil war broke out across the Macedonian Empire, eventually leading to its disintegration.

The challenge when Jobs died was how to protect the palace. I think we can agree that Apple has more than risen to the challenge. Jobs was a disruptor, challenger and conqueror. He exploded category after category, overturning the establishment in each, whether it was computers, phones, watches, mobile payments, photography, music or instant messaging. He took territory far beyond the company's original patch. When he sadly died, it was reasonable to think a fate similar to Alexander's would befall his empire, with the generals of Silicon Valley not knowing what to do. However, what current Apple CEO Tim Cook has done is miraculous. He taught his empire how to protect the palace, and in doing so answered the most critical challenge facing an insurgent: How the rebel becomes the warrior. Rebels overturn the establishment, and as Apple has gone on to become the establishment, it is now a kingdom of warriors living to protect it. And doing an excellent job of it.

3.2

LEADER

If the emotional effect a brand wants to create is status, then you adopt a Leader Brand Role. Status is powerful emotional territory. It means that your consumers can literally say of themselves, in pure Darwinian terms, *"Procreate with me. I'm a good hunter; your children won't go hungry."* It's all about conveying conspicuous wealth. The effect of status is delivered when your brand's place is at the heart of the establishment. You are the leader of the establishment. You have arrived, your ritual is that of influence, and your time means authority. You have rational values that orient around stability, prosperity and protection, and they're augmented by the emotional values of tradition, prestige and power. You stand for strength and are against weakness.

We see that leaders in culture are a potent force. It is Vito Corleone in *The Godfather*, Nelson Mandela in *Invictus*, Queen Elizabeth in *The Crown*, Winston Churchill in *The Darkest Hour* and Daenerys Targaryen in *Game of Thrones*. All of them have narratives of power, authority and admiration. They are all protectors, but they're also bestowers of great generosity. We see these attributes in leader brands such as Rolls Royce, Moët Chandon, Patek Philippe, Barclays and Mercedes Benz. They are all brands of destination. They're keepers of tradition, objects of admiration, signifiers of power and authority. They are protectors, and they are also beacons of generosity and abundance. It is a powerful archetype, but it's ultimately the leader of the establishment.

If you are representing the establishment, you're bestowing status onto your consumers.

You can innovate into the role of leader, which shifts and changes in culture but, ultimately, a leader position becomes a defensive position. It becomes a lofty perch where you don't have to take risks to try and win, and you don't lose. It is more of a *playing not to lose* scenario, one of maintaining the status quo, which is tough, because there are lots of challenger brands out there.

The advantage of being in a Leader Brand Role is that people fall into your slipstream, and if you're bigger than everybody else, they aim to replicate you. The disadvantage is the lack of agility, hobbling your ability to readily move and shift. The leader does not have the facility to shape shift in order to create new space, which is what the challengers have.

3.3 CHILD

The Child Brand Role archetype is the meaning system you deploy to effect wonder. We get there by rooting the brands in the place of magic, in the rituals of play and at a time of fantasy. The rational values of a Child Brand are possibility, simplicity and creativity. The emotional values are innocence, curiosity and imagination. What we stand for in this role is The Limitless, and what we stand against is The Limited. In terms of culture, it's Luna Lovegood in *Harry Potter*, Elliot in *ET*, Josh Baskin in *Big*, Forrest Gump, Lucy in *The Chronicles of Narnia*.

The role of the child is all about shifting the ordinary to the extraordinary. It's about revelling in beauty and innocence. This narrative goes beyond the limits, exploring one's imagination, having childlike wisdom and innocence. Some of the biggest global brands inhabit the Child Role. We see it in Lego, Sony Bravia, Haribo and Disney. They convey the notion of being extraordinary, of beauty, of having no limits, of imagination.

That wide-eyed sense of wonder is something that most adults lose as we get older. A philosopher once said that we're so deeply entrenched in our routines and habits that it sometimes takes observing a child, watching them play, to remind yourself of the joy in that innocence and that curiosity, and the fact that we can take ourselves too seriously. To some extent, it is about unlearning. *"It took me four years to paint like Raphael,"* Picasso was quoted as saying, *"but a lifetime to paint like a child."*

This is a wonderful role for a brand, dispensing fun and laughter, which is can be such a refreshing tonic. A bit of joy nurtures and maintains the soul, which is a lovely archetype for a brand to adopt.

3.4

GUIDE

The Guide Role is the opposite of childlike inspiration. One way to look at the segue from child to guide can be through Star Wars. In the first film, Obi-Wan Kenobi is guide and mentor to an almost childlike Luke Skywalker. In later installations, Luke would complete his training and become Grand Master. In ancient mythology, we see the centaur Chiron, a half-man, half-horse, in this role, tutoring Greek heroes. He possessed the intuition of an animal and the intellect of a human. Chiron spent 40 years in the wilderness, honing the hunting and survival instincts of a beast while amassing human wisdom that encompassed medicine, astronomy, philosophy and music. When the gods went to war, they thought he would be quite an asset, and put him on the battlefield, where he overcame everybody. This prompted them to send their children, including Hercules and Achilles, to be schooled by Chiron in the art of warfare.

This resonates when you think about the themes of being in balance with nature, and the wisdom of the natural world, and deploying that through martial arts. We can see elements of that in the Jedi or ninja, and the heroic (and anti-hero) depictions in Hollywood. It is as much Gandalf in *The Lord of the Rings* as it is Obi-Wan Kenobi in *Star Wars*.

The effect of this role is immensely powerful. It's the effect of empowerment, giving you the magic of trusting yourself. The place is transformation. The ritual is that of preparation. The time is the time of challenge. The rational values are to inspire, mentor and encourage with emotional values and perspective, becoming more experienced and more intuitive. In terms of charisma, this brand type stands for fulfilment and potential, and it stands against being unfulfilled.

A great female version of the Guide Role is Luana Johnson in *Dangerous Minds*. It's Brendan in *Sing Street* and Mr Han in *Karate Kid*. In all those films, there is the imparting of knowledge, leading by example, accepting mistakes, the uncovering of the latent hero and a journey of perspective. We see that in brands such as Microsoft, This Girl Can, Hyundai, Beats and Headspace. They all use the narratives of imparting wisdom, leading by example, being accepting, uncovering the path and revealing new perspectives.

This is a strong role, and it's obvious why educational institutions or learning apps would adopt the archetype of the guide.

Another example of the Guide Role is pop-culture adventurer Bear Grylls. As we've touched on, he was a Special Forces soldier, the youngest Brit to climb Everest, and went on to become a survival expert, writer and death-defying television personality. On the face of it, he's a warrior, an adventurer, or both. But we recognised that as he was getting older, we could future-proof his brand by moving him into the role of The Guide. His scars and weathered countenance are testament to battles won, and he returns to impart his wisdom. As former Chief Scout in the UK and then Chief Ambassador of World Scouting, he has helped design and guide the youth movement's programming, brand relationships and partnerships.

Another brand I worked on is the Australian sports compression-wear company 2XU. Nike personifies the individual, and Adidas the team, which meant we had two places to go: the fan or the coach. We built 2XU's brand role as that of the coach, pushing for marginal gains. Tight-fitting compression apparel applies pressure to the body, increasing blood flow, helping muscles perform more efficiently and reducing exercise fatigue. To the athlete, this means training harder and recovering more quickly. Train hard, play easy. It came down to positioning 2XU in this trainer/manager role, pivoting off notion of The Guide. It's Al Pacino in *Any Given Sunday*, coaching the Miami Sharks football team.

3.5

PURIST

The Purist Brand archetype is becoming more and more powerful, with more brands adopting it, especially in the fashion sector.

The purist ideal in archetypal terms is Atalanta, a heroine in Greek mythology. She was a huntress who turned her back on the palace, went to live in the wilderness and became a skilled survivalist. It was said that she could run through a forest without disturbing a bird or breaking a twig, and she was a better hunter than all her male folk. She was incredibly beautiful, and many wanted to marry her. It was agreed that she would only marry a suitor who could outrun her in a foot race. If unsuccessful, a contestant would be killed. Many aspirants died in the attempt.

The effect of the Purist Brand Role is authenticity. The place is the place of self-belief, and the ritual is of self-sufficiency. The time of this brand is self-reliance. In terms of rational values, it is self-referential, it is truthful and it is free. Its emotional values are intuitive, independent and instinctive. The authenticity of the effect arises from its charisma, which comes from standing for being original, and staunchly against the unoriginal. In many ways, this brand will have a profound effect on the culture it's not in. It will stand apart from mainstream culture and represent the parallel universe of doing things your own way, as an agent of change and influential outsider. In cultural terms, this is Don Draper in *Mad Men*.

As a female version of purist in literary terms, she is Bathsheba Everdene in the book *Far from the Madding Crowd*, a character who inspired the Hunger Games character Katniss Everdeen. It is Jim Stark in the movie *Rebel Without a Cause*. However, this is not a Rebel Brand Role, in that they aren't trying to overturn something. It is a rebel brand without a cause. It's about being truly you, and who you really are. It's Wolverine in *X-Men*, Merida in *Brave* and Maya in *Zero Dark Thirty*.

In terms of the narrative, it demands respect because it has an alignment of single purpose. It is on the outside, so it sets its own context. It is free-spirited, it is passionate, and it generates the most important freedom of all, which is to be who you are, to be original. The brands that project this persona are Guinness, Adidas Originals, New Balance and Dove. They are outside the normal context, they are free-spirited, they live life with passionate intensity. That's a powerful archetype. It could, in fact, be hard to live up to. It is a brand role where you have to be fully committed and own it. This brand is going to do things its own way. You don't set a business objective and try to meet the number; you set a behavioural objective for the purists out there, and the numbers take care of themselves.

3.6 ADVENTURER

The emotional effect you are trying to create with the Adventurer Brand Role is exhilaration. When we use the products and absorb the communication, the feeling we should get is the thrill of an adrenaline rush. It comes from landing the brand in a place of the unexplored, stepping off the map and venturing into the unknown. It is the ritual of exploration and the time of pioneering. It is rooted in the rational values of being adaptable, of persevering, of openness, all wrapped up in resilience but propelled by the emotional values of ambition, fearlessness, curiosity and of going where no one's been before. This is a brand whose charisma comes from standing for the unknown and standing against the known.

It is not a brand role or a system for the faint-hearted. In cultural terms, this is Indiana Jones, Francois in *The Beach*,

Cooperin *Interstellar*, Philippe Petit in *The Walk*, and in *Game of Thrones*, it is Arya Stark. It is a brand whose narratives are insatiable curiosity, a desire to brave the unknown, a need to go on a quest to test oneself. It's a fearlessness in taking on and never backing down from whatever's in front of you, of being durable on these enduring adventures and never being frightened by danger. The closer we get to danger, the more we learn about ourselves. In brand terms, it is Land Rover, and The North Face, with its Never Stop Exploring ethos. It is a GoPro, the Omega in Space watches, and it's the Danish butter brand Lurpak. More recently, Marks and Spencer's foods have ventured into this space too, pivoting to the Adventurer Role archetype, to explore the unknown, be curious, follow the quest, show fearlessness, adapt to danger.

This is a really wonderful brand image. I've worked with it a lot, and it has become more in demand after COVID-19. During the pandemic lockdowns and deprivations, people wanted to either be equipped to handle the reality of their situation or inspired to escape it. It was during that period that we helped Burberry play off this as a brand platform. We also helped outdoor clothing and footwear purveyor Montane pivot here too. It became very prevalent in our work because of the notion of being idealistic and escaping reality.

COVID-19 had an interesting psychological impact on brand identity. When we were all in lockdown, and our horizons suddenly shortened quite abruptly and forcefully, the desire to step into the unknown was far more attractive. As such, this adventurous brand role provided an antidote to our reduced freedoms and diminished horizons.

We researched the narratives that people consumed during trying times, including looking at the Best Picture winners at the Oscars throughout the last century during times of crisis. During the First World War, the Great Depression, WWII, the Cuban Missile Crisis and Vietnam, up through to the 2007–08 credit crisis.

Across that arc, there were two types of films that people gravitated towards. One thematic thread was idealism, such as in *The Wizard of Oz*, or realism, as seen in *Dr. Strangelove* or *The Killing Fields*. People sought out either realistic narratives or idealistic storylines during difficult periods.

The challenge for companies during troublesome times is which to be: a realistic brand, helping people deal with the situation, or an idealistic one, helping them escape their situation. Or you can try and combine the two, where you might have an idealistic narrative with a realistic treatment. Think: *Rocky*. This film, which won five Oscars, has a classic idealistic narrative but with a realistic delivery. *Avatar* represents the opposite, the inverse of a realistic narrative, with the murdering of indigenous populations dressed up in a cartoon.

3.7 TRICKSTER

The Trickster Brand Role is the meaning system to adopt to create the effect of unbridled joy. Joy found in the place of chaos, in the ritual of upheaval, in the time of disorder. The trickster character, who has appeared across various cultures through history, is an excited, witty, disruptive archetype. Its rational values are restlessness, opportunistic and irreverence, augmented by the emotional values of humorous, audacious and mischievous. This role stands for unpredictability. It is a really volatile, chaotic persona and quite interesting when you consider that the direction of time is demonstrably from order to chaos.

Einstein may have had other theoretical ideas, but we all know what direction time travels in. If you put an apple on your desk, it decays. It's the same with houses — they don't become more modernised but instead fade into restoration projects. And, of course, we age too. Our once lithe, youthful body becomes increasingly enfeebled as we get older. We, therefore, know that the direction of time is from order to disorder, and this is a brand role that celebrates that.

In film culture, it is Jack Sparrow in *Pirates of the Caribbean*, and in *Beverly Hills Cop*, it's Axel Foley. It's also the mischievously brilliant Ferris in *Ferris Bueller's Day Off*, Fred and George Weasley in *Harry Potter*, and in many ways it is Villanelle in *Killing Eve*. Those in this role really push boundaries. They have a lightness of foot, and they revel in wreaking havoc. They are a catalyser of chaos and impulsive but exude great charm. They have the narratives of skirting boundaries and stirring up trouble and yet are appealing in a naughty sort of way. This is seen in Cadbury's, Mini, Old Spice; it's there in M&Ms and felt in IKEA.

You can see how this is a way of conveying some very powerful narratives as we move through time. The Trickster Brand Role embodies escapism and delight, wicked humour, the ability to laugh in the face of chaos. These brands do the unexpected, don't necessarily know where they're going, and when they go tangentially off script and do something unexpected, we follow in awe and wonder. It's a potent brand role to choose, but you have to be able to back it all up — you can't create this role and have a boring product.

3.8 CRAFTSMAN

The Craftsman Brand Role is one of the most dominant product personas, especially when the brand has been founder-led, and that founder is an artisan. This becomes a natural place to go, and elicits the brand effect of trust. Trust in the products you use, and knowing that the brand you're consuming has your back on a micro level, so you can trust yourselves on a macro level.

The place of this brand is the place of inspiration; it is the ritual of creation and the time of patience. You can't rush craftsmanship.

The values rationally are diligence, innovation and mastery. The emotional values are perfection and passion, but marshalled by humility. This is a brand that stands for perfection and is decidedly against imperfection.

In terms of culture, it is a secondary player in socio-cultural narratives. It's very much in the background, with the product taking centre stage. In film culture, this is Q, the quartermaster in *James Bond*, or sword maker Hattori Hanzō in *Kill Bill*. It's John Baptiste in *Perfume*, the tech whizz Shuri in *Black Panther*, or Gendry, the blacksmith in *Game of Thrones*. The narratives that they all have are oriented around trust; you must trust the process to make the object of craftsmanship. That will, in turn, inspire intuitive performance on the part of the warrior, who is being bestowed with the object.

This requires patience, because you can't rush craftsmanship. It requires intuition. It is about having mastery over the detail and the associated trust in the craftsmanship. Whether it's the engineering from Germany or precision from Switzerland, it's all closely tied to place. In brands, it is the camera and lens maker Leica, it is Honda, it is Cartier, and it is Jack Daniels. You can see in these brands that they are centred on the process of creativity, the performance of the product, the patience that goes into the handcrafting, the intuition it creates, the detail they evangelise and the locale of creation. This is a remarkably powerful role, when the magic of the brand is in the very essence of the product.

Sometimes, craftsman gets blended. We can use Craftsman Brand Role narratives for product communication and then augment that with the personality from another. I have done Warrior Craftsman at Volvo with Arquus, Rebel Craftsman at Mountain Equipment.

I believe that the craftsman persona comes into its own when you have a large and varied consumer base, with different demographics over different geographies. When you're looking for something that can work across several different areas (a Venn diagram with lots of circles), the craftsman is an excellent brand to use.

3.9

WARRIOR

The Warrior Brand Role is equipped by the Craftsman, empowered by the Guide and serving the Leader. This is an important role because the greatest of brands usually reconcile anxiety. Anxiety exists in the consumer psyche, and it is no mistake that most teenagers will have a pair of Nikes in their wardrobe. This is because they'll generally have a crisis of confidence at some point regarding their identity, and one of the roles of a brand is to fill that gap in our character. Nike is the Warrior brand, conjuring the effect of confidence. If there is a crisis of self-confidence, then this is the brand for you. It's why many teenagers continue to wear Nike.

Confidence comes from the place of battle. Whether that battle is walking into a classroom or a meeting room, it's that product, in that place, that gives you confidence. It embodies the rituals of achievement, and the time that you own is that of triumph. The rational values of this role are discipline, excellence and determination, and they bring with them the emotional values of honour, prowess and courage. The charisma and conviction from this brand come from standing for victory and against defeat.

It is famously portrayed in film culture through Maximus Decimus Meridius in *Gladiator*. It is Ripley in *Alien*, Maggie in *Million Dollar Baby*, T'Challa in *Black Panther* and, perhaps most famously of all, it's James Bond in *Skyfall* (and all the *James Bond* films).

This is a brand that represents a protector of the establishment. Warriors don't live very long, so they live in the present. But that doesn't mean that the brand should burn white-hot and fizzle out quickly. It is merely a stance to take — that you're willing to go into battle on behalf of the establishment, to protect people.

It is all about living in the moment and having mastery in skill and prowess. It's about rituals and narratives of preparation. It is being so skilful that the sword becomes an extension of your arm, so it's an intuitive appendage. It is also about the spoils of victory. In brands, it's Nike, Under Armour, BMW, Lucozade and the Royal Marines. As brands, they communicate that they are there to protect the orthodoxy and the establishment, in the present. This is a strong role that creates a brand system, giving confidence and reconciling anxiety. Companies need to choose whether they are a brand of destination or a brand of transition. A brand of destination is one we consume when we've arrived. A brand of transition is one we journey through life with. In automotive terms, someone might travel through Audi to arrive at Mercedes. So in that situation, Audi is the transitory brand, and Mercedes is the destination brand. In luggage terms, we might travel through Louis Vuitton to get to Goyard or to Hermes.

Warrior brands represent transition, in a process of continual reinvention. Think Nike, whose cohort is 16 to 24 year olds. People move on — they move beyond Nike and into All Birds, etc. This means that Nike has to continually reinvent what it means to be 16–24, and they do that by being the Warrior, a source of continual inspiration. This is demonstrated by the company's athlete endorsements. Like warriors, they don't live forever and have to be recycled, as seen by the early figures Nike sponsored: Steve Prefontaine was followed by Jimmy Connors, McEnroe, Nâstaze, Agassi, Jordan and Kobe. All Nike endorsers have their time, and then the brand moves on with the times, having to continually reinvent itself.

3.10

GUARDIAN

Closely related to the Warrior is the Guardian Brand Role, and the emotional effect is not confidence but protection. If you want your consumer to feel protected by your communication and protected by using your products, then choose the Guardian persona. The place of the Guardian is the place of safety. It is the ritual of nurturing, and it is the time of vulnerability. The Guardian's rational values are stability, support and selflessness. The emotional values are strength, compassion and love. This brand stands for security and stands against insecurity.

In film culture, we love this brand. It is Mary Poppins or Marlin in *Finding Nemo*. It is Leigh Anne Tuohy in *The Blind Side*, Ben Cash in *Captain Fantastic* and Mrs Weasley in *Harry Potter*. The narratives are maternal love, protection, paternal comfort, living in balance, of being nourished and of nurturing. These are evidenced in the brands we consume that adopt the Guardian role. Obvious ones like Johnson & Johnson, Volvo, Coleman's, Procter & Gamble and the Center Parcs holiday getaway service all use the narratives of love, protection, comfort, balance, nourishment and nurturing. It's a reassuringly strong role when it comes to family-oriented products.

It's possible to inject a little bit of excitement into a brand within the Guardian Brand Role. Volvo is one of the most credible brands on the planet and has achieved that through a product expression of safety that enables you to go and do things that are extraordinary. The Volvo 'Stuntman' ad from the early 1990s was powerful and exciting, and the automaker still benefits from it, telegraphing the image of a sturdy yet stylish conveyance that protects you in extreme circumstances.

3.11

PARTNER

The emotional effect of the Partner Brand Role is support. This comes from positioning the brand in a place of affinity, with the rituals of kinship, of 'being in it together.' The rational values this brand uses as a platform are that it is straightforward, supportive and dependable. The emotional values are loyalty, compassion and generosity. It represents togetherness and stands against loneliness. These two components combine to project a great depth of charisma.

We find this culturally in some of the most wonderful films and stories. It is Butch in *Butch Cassidy and the Sundance Kid*, Thelma and Louise, Samwise Gamgee in *The Lord of the Rings*, Dory in *Finding Nemo*, Annie in *Bridesmaids*, and Woody in *Toy Story*.

This is a brand that uses narratives of going beyond distinctions. It's about attachment and shared experiences, of being the sum rather than the part. It has the rituals of togetherness and the reassurance of forming bonds of trust. It's demonstrated by the 'We All Belong' campaign for Airbnb. It is very clear in Coca-Cola, teaching the world to sing in perfect harmony during the Vietnam War, followed by the 'Mean Joe Greene' football player spots during a time of racial unrest in America. Coke came out with tender-hearted counterpoints to what was happening in society and politics, providing important cultural moments that people rallied around. They've become iconic in the brand's advertising history. Other examples include J.Crew, Vodafone and 'We're all in it together,' with the black horses of Lloyds Bank. The Partner Role is a really potent brand system for engendering a sense of togetherness and support. It has been more in demand in the last few years, given Gen Z's 'community and belonging' vibe, perhaps born out of the forced isolation of the COVID-19 pandemic.

3.12

LOVER

Here, we examine the Lover Brand Role. It's really the effect of temptation and desire. We find it in the place of decadence, in the ritual of being unrestrained, and in the time of ecstasy. The Lover's brand is based on rational values of being uninhibited, celebrating beauty and charm. Those are underpinned by the emotional values of sensuality, spontaneity and indulging in pleasure. It's standing for self-indulgence and against self-denial.

The role in cinema is portrayed by Satine, the Nicole Kidman character in *Moulin Rouge!*, Jessica Rabbit in *Who Framed Roger Rabbit*, Romeo and Juliet, Rose in *Titanic*, and Jacob Palmer in *Crazy, Stupid, Love*. These are all based around the narratives of want, especially when something's forbidden or when it's lost. It speaks to being irresistible, sensual and feasting on joy. Being desired and desiring at the same time. It exists in brands like Chanel, Lacoste, Galaxy, Häagen-Dazs and Virgin, who all strive to communicate the narratives of forbidden want, irresistibility, the senses and feasting.

It was Oscar Wilde who said, *"I can resist everything except temptation."* The brand that best epitomised this was Gucci in the '90s and early 2000s, when Tom Ford was Creative Director. It was the Lover Brand Role on drugs, a full-on, phenomenal exposition of the idea of the lover.

3.13

VISIONARY

The Visionary Brand Role is one you would choose if you wanted the effect of your product to be optimism. It goes to a hopefulness that enables seeing new possibilities, having a positive impact on societies and inspiring a better future. It is an important role whose ritual is reimagining the possible. The time is that of a new dawn, and the place is new horizons. These are underpinned by the core rational values of innovation, intuition and potential and the emotional values of empowerment, idealism and conviction.

In terms of driving conviction and charisma, the Visionary stands for the possible and against the impossible. Nothing is impossible with the Visionary. It's all unbridled optimism, driving the endlessly possible.

If you were to choose this brand in popular culture, it's Steve Jobs in the film of the same title, Stephen Hawking in *The Theory of Everything*, and Abe Lincoln in the biopic *Lincoln*. It is also Alan Turing in *The Imitation Game* and Catherine Johnson in *Hidden Figures*.

The narratives culturally are those of foresight, being able to think conceptually, having a passion for society, being ready to start a small revolution in the name of freedom, following through with conviction. In brands, we would see it as being Tesla, CoinCloud, Honda, Netflix and Virgin Galactic. They offer narratives of foresight, conceptual thinking, compassion, revolutionary freedom and conviction. The Visionary is the brand for the bold and the brave.

I would advise a company to consider Visionary for a new or existing product that was demonstrably superior to everything already available. Once you can identify a gap between the competition and your product in terms of functional superiority, you can consider pursuing Visionary as a strong persona to align the product with.

Without technical and/or performance superiority, the Visionary Band Role could ring hollow, unless there were other functions it fulfilled. For example, it could refer to social or cultural impacts, as we see with Toms. The company's shoes aren't necessarily a visionary product, and are not functionally better than everybody else's, but for every pair bought, they give one to help people in need. In this way, they fulfil a Visionary Brand Role, with emotional superiority. A brand can be Visionary in marketing if not necessarily in product or service.

3.14

TRIBE

The Tribe Brand Role is a meaning system you'd choose if the effect you want is one of belonging. The Tribe persona lets consumers feel part of something bigger than themselves, a sense of pride, self-belief and confidence in their own capabilities. It seeks a sense of individual identity but set within a wider collective. It speaks to the very human urge to belong. The ritual of the Tribe is the ritual of learned experiences; it is the time of teamship and the friendly place of kith and kin. These are underpinned by rational values of respect, openness and equality, with the emotional values being honour, inclusivity and generosity, which, when brought together, deliver the effect of affinity and affection.

The Tribe stands for loyalty — loyalty to the commune — and stands against disloyalty, creating feelings of conviction and charisma.

In TV and film, we see this in the show *Friends*, and more recently in *Nomadland*, which pulled us into the tribe of recession-battered travellers led by Fern. *Captain Fantastic* was about the familiar tribe, and *Stranger Things* and *This Is Us* were demonstrative of the tribal group through time.

All of these cultural entities have common narratives: the customs of the tribal collective, the agency it gives to its members, the group's continual reinvention, love, commitment and acceptance, as well as the construct's relatable imperfections.

In brands, we would see that as being Airbnb, Coca-Cola, Mini, Android and Starbucks, all of which have elements of customs, agency, reinvention, communitas, commitment and acceptance.

The Tribe has to signify and symbolise from the centre and abdicate actions to the edges. You don't have to curate or edit who's in and who's out of the group. From a brand perspective, that's taken care of through what you symbolise and signify.

One of the best exponents of this in street culture was Stussy, the California surf and skate brand, which represented a certain kind of freedom. Those who gravitated to it weren't necessarily surfers and skaters. They were graffiti artists, hip-hop artists and cool kids of every stripe, who were drawn to the laid-back, free-spirited Stussy Tribe.

3.15
EVERYMAN

The Everyman Brand Role has the emotional effect of truth. It is instilled with honesty, integrity and a sense of fairness. A particularly strong belief in fairness. It is working on behalf of the common good; it is speaking up for what is right, especially on behalf of others and it's instilled with a sense of pride and purpose.

The core ritual of Everyman is seeing through pretence. It is the time of honesty; it is the place of universality. Adherents stand for reality and stand against fantasy. The core values rationally are tradition, toil and equality. Core values emotionally are humility, honesty and integrity. They all add up to this effect of truth.

In film and TV, Rocky Balboa is Everyman personified. *Fleabag*, Forrest Gump, Dai Donovan in *Pride* and Mare in *Mare of Easttown* share the narrative of authenticity, being human, realism, value, belonging to and supporting a collective, and being genuinely exceptional.

In brands, this is Volkswagen, Heinz, Carhartt and Yorkshire Tea. They exude authenticity and human realism and value the collective group.

The reason luxury exists is to confer status on the consumer. I have not seen it done, though it would be interesting to see how Everyman can be applied to luxury brands, which may not be compatible with conferring a grassroots truth. We see Everyman evident in household products such as the wood stain Ronseal.

It says what it does on the tin. Those are the attributes of truth and straightforwardness.

3.16 ANTI-HERO

Last but by no means least is the Anti-Hero Brand Role, which is special because it is relatively new. One of the things in storytelling that has accelerated our absorption of archetypes is the rise of media streaming, with virtual box-set bingeing and the ability to connect in a much deeper way with characters. If we look at 5,000 years of human history, storytelling started with the spoken word around a campfire. Fast forward to the last 100 years, and we have the invention of cinema and greater accessibility to mass-culture storytelling. We might have seen a film once a month, and perhaps a play every six months. Now, we can access films every day through TV or on our laptop, with a multitude of streaming options. And this acceleration in the consumption of storytelling has give new rise to the archetype, the Anti-Hero. Walter White (*Breaking Bad*), Tony Soprano (*The Sopranos*), *Money Heist*, *Deadpool* and Harley Quinn in *Birds of Prey*. Consistent with all anti-heroes is a deep sense of integrity, and though they may be deeply flawed, there's the feeling that their heart's in the right place. We love them despite their imperfections and will follow them if we think they have a good heart.

All of these characters have the narratives of controversy, redemption, being unrestrained, being impulsive, demonstrating moral contrast and in some way being conflicted. This is new white space with respect to meaning systems. A critic in Hollywood said, *"Not since Hamlet has anybody written a character with the tapestry and texture and depth of Tony Soprano."*

The Anti-Hero conveys the effect of being uninhibited. They're at ease with their flaws and fallibilities and are released from certain moral and legal constraints. They stand for breaking the rules; they stand against following the rules. Their ritual is one I love: Embracing the dark side. We need night and shade. You don't really understand someone's character until you've seen the Jekyll and Hyde in them. It is the ritual of knowing the extent of their dark side, watching through knit-together fingers, taking perverse delight in it. Their time is the right time to embrace the dark side, and the place of the Anti-Hero is to be in the wrong place at the right time.

Their core emotional and rational values are interesting. Rationally, they're about provocation and imperfection, and because we can see in them our own imperfections, we fall in love with them. They have a code of integrity that's slightly warped vis-à-vis the conventions of normal life, but it makes sense in their life. The Anti-Hero Brand Role delivers the emotional values of autonomy, freedom and defiance. All of them add up to being uninhibited.

Though not that evident in today's brands, this persona can be glimpsed in '90s Benetton, Harley Davidson, Palace Skateboards and perhaps in Diesel. All revelled in elements of controversy and redemption, of being slightly unrestrained, impulsive and dark. In some way, they exist to shine a light on the conflict between the raw and the civilised. It is an intriguing role that we have not yet fully seen play out in a global brand, on a grand scale.

The concept of the anti-hero, deeply rooted in American cultural consciousness through the western genre, has found a powerful contemporary expression in the political arena. Many voters in recent American elections, particularly those of an older generation, were raised on Wild West narratives that often featured a flawed protagonist who would arrive to set things right in a troubled town, to remedy the official authorities' ineffectiveness.

This archetype, with its acceptance of morally ambiguous methods in pursuit of a perceived greater good, has been skilfully leveraged in modern politics. Donald Trump's campaign strategy exemplifies this approach, positioning him as an outsider ready to 'drain the swamp' in Washington. His promise to clean up the political establishment and then depart echoes the familiar trajectory of the western anti-hero. Think Clint Eastwood in *High Plains Drifter*, among many others.

Trump's political brand deliberately taps into this simple yet evocative storytelling tradition. He employs straightforward, accessible language, avoiding complex political jargon in favour of catchy phrases and memorably crass nicknames for opponents (Crooked Hillary, Sleepy Joe, Little Marco, Lyin' Kamala, Meatball Ron), essentially making cartoon characters out of them. This transforms political discourse into a narrative more akin to a nursery rhyme, making it easily digestible for a wide audience.

The effectiveness of this strategy underscores the enduring power of storytelling in shaping public opinion and even altering the course of history. It demonstrates how deeply ingrained narrative structures can influence political outcomes, sometimes with far-reaching consequences.

Trump and his sort notwithstanding, having an understanding these storytelling mechanisms is key in driving positive change, not just in politics but also in business and socio-economic spheres. By recognising and responsibly wielding the power of narrative, we can potentially guide societal progress towards a more constructive and sustainable future rather than a destructive one. This awareness of storytelling's impact is key to ensuring that our collective journey leads to regeneration and improvement rather than degradation and decline.

And along the way, we will get some 'pinch yourself' moments.

> "I REALISED MY PROMISE TO MYSELF HAD BEEN REALISED. I'D MADE MOUNTAIN LIFE A PART OF MY LIFE."

PINCH YOURSELF MOMENTS

ANNECY

In my mid-20s I had my first ski trip to the French Alps. I begged, borrowed and stole awful clothing, mainly C&A Rodeo gear. I rented equipment, gave it my best, but quickly realised that I couldn't ski. It simply wasn't for me.

I sat on the snow and watched elegant women and handsome men glide past, looking down at me with sympathy and a little distain.

I was angry that I'd never been to the mountains before, but I made a promise to myself that I'd make this part of my life, somehow, because despite my awful skiing and terrible clothing, I loved being there. I loved the feeling of awe that the mountains inspired.

Within a few years, I had managed to become Creative Director of mountaineering brand Karrimor, and from there co-founded FreshBritain. Winning the Nike ACG contract enabled me to live in the mountains for six months and invest the time and effort necessary to become a proficient and elegant snowboarder.

While living in the Haute-Savoie, and in no small part because of the work we'd done on Nike, we were selected to redesign the Salomon brand. Residing in the French Alps, you realise just what a privilege and honour it is for the people who live there to work on a brand like Salomon.

It was through the Salomon job that I realised my promise to myself had been realised. I'd made mountain life a part of my life.

Walking through the doors of the company's headquarters in Annecy was truly a 'pinch yourself' moment.

SQUAMISH

When I was Creative Director at Karrimor, I wanted to take the 'clean' visual aesthetic of the parallel universe that was snowboarding and apply it to what was then the often lurid aesthetic of mountaineering clothing.

We launched the refreshed product range at a trade show in Utah in the late 1990s, and it was there that I first came across Arc'teryx. Wow.

They too had adopted a clean aesthetic, but they combined this with three-dimensional articulation, waterproof zips and sonic seam welding. This all meant that their product was not just ahead of my product, it was a seismic paradigm shift in clothing design. It was the clothing version of the launch of the iPhone. Absolutely amazing. I was blown away.

Fast forward a decade, and I was invited to redesign the Arc'teryx brand, to help get them from $100 million to $1 billion but keep them special.

Arriving in Squamish, British Columbia, along the spectacularly ascending Sea to Sky Highway, and walking into Arc'teryx headquarters to meet the leadership team and help redesign what was already an incredible brand was another unbelievable 'pinch yourself' moment.

HILVERSUM

When I was 14 years old, I used to hang around on a BMX bike with the Duffy family. The Duffys were well known in the BMX universe, as Donna was number four in the world, and Jason and Ash were in the top 10. They all used to ride for the Hutch factory team. They were all incredibly cool.

It was on them that I first saw the swoosh logo. They were

wearing blue and orange Nike waffle racers. That was also the first time I saw a cool sneaker that wasn't Adidas or Vans.

Fast forward a few decades, and I was invited to the Dutch city of Hilversum to embark on a project to redesign Nike's ACG action sports brand. The category had evolved from core action sports like BMX.

4. BRAND PRACTICE

4.1 STORYTELLING

This section explores the intricate relationship between brand design, product design and communication design, emphasising the importance of storytelling across all mediums. The key to success lies in creating a unified brand narrative that seamlessly integrates rational and emotional values into both product creation and communication strategies.

Rather than viewing these elements as separate entities, we should view them as different conduits through which we tell the same brand story. I learned this approach as Creative Director at Converse and later in that role at outdoor brand Karrimor, where I oversaw all communications in addition to product design. These comprehensive roles highlighted the importance of a single narrative — how a single brand story could be conveyed through different channels, from material selection in product design to casting choices in advertisements.

The essence of effective storytelling in both product and communication design revolves around two primary goals: making people think and making them feel. The 'thinking' aspect aims to create awareness and understanding of the product or message, while the 'feeling' component seeks to establish a personal connection, linking back to the consumer's sense of self.

This concept aligns with how individuals define themselves, either through statements of being ('I am') or doing ('I do'). Effective storytelling in design and communication taps into both aspects of identity. It makes people aware of what a product or brand does (thinking) and believe in its value (feeling), connecting with both their sense of action and identity.

In product design, this translates to creating items that consumers perceive as functional — it's an obedient product, and will do what it is designed to do — while also incorporating cues that foster a sense of belonging to a particular group or tribe. In communication design, every choice, from visual elements to messaging, carries meaning and consequences, contributing to the overall narrative.

For me, two influential figures shaped this understanding. One was Hervé Bertrand, one of the best product designers in the world, a master of storytelling through form, construction and material in product design. The other was Rachel Thomas, an artist who emphasised that every design choice, or lack thereof, has meaning and consequences. Both worked with FreshBritain, and both taught me a huge amount, including the importance of storytelling and meaningful choice.

This section underscores the importance of making meaningful choices in design and communication. By carefully considering each decision and its impact on the overall brand story, we can create a cohesive narrative that resonates with consumers rationally and emotionally, spanning all touchpoints of the brand experience.

4.2 PRODUCT DESIGN

Product design is a multifaceted discipline that requires a deep understanding of how various elements combine to create a thing that not only functions as intended but also resonates with consumers on both rational and emotional levels. The key to successful product design lies in recognising and leveraging two key components that make us think about its functionality and feel a sense of belonging or connection to it.

Four primary elements contribute to our perception of a product's functionality: form, construction, technology and material. The 'form language' of a product should immediately convey its purpose. For instance, a Caterpillar Earth Moving Machine's form suggests durability, while a Ferrari's sleek lines evoke speed and a Ducati delivers irrepressibility. In cars it is all about styling, with the form language designed to cover up engineering, whereas in motorbikes it is design to conspicuously reveal the engineering.

Construction language also plays a crucial role in shaping our thoughts about a product. For example, Arc'teryx's sonic welding technique communicates a progressive, future-facing approach, whereas Hublot watches make you think they're bomb-proof.

Technological language is equally important in conveying a product's capabilities. Nike Air technology suggests lightweight performance, while Salomon's XT Wings trail running shoes used an anatomical design language to communicate their ability to handle challenging terrains. The language layering for the trail running shoe was anatomically familiar. When you picked it up, you saw that it had an external framework we called 'skeleton.' We gave it cushioning technology that was called 'muscle,' and designed a lacing system we called 'tendons.' In the store, people could look at the shoe design, associate it with the biomorphic language and immediately understand it, contributing to its huge sales numbers. Assigning technical language to one of the rational values is critical to success.

The material language of a product can also significantly influence our perception, making us think and connect. Levi's denim, for instance, speaks to authenticity and personal history. It says something about the character of the product and the wearer; a material that tells my story through what I wear.

Speedo's shark skin-inspired fabric conveys speed and adaptive ease of movement through your environment.

On the emotional side, elements such as branding, patterns, textures and colours contribute to our sense of belonging to a product or its associated tribe. These often represent codes that we subconsciously interpret. For example, brown shoes might signify an outdoor lifestyle, black boots were traditionally safety wear, and white trainers are historically associated with tennis.

To create a comprehensive product design, it's essential to establish a set of brand values and apply them strategically to these design components. Typically, three rational values are assigned to the elements that make us think (through the design components form, construction, technology and material), while three emotional values are applied to the elements that make us feel (via the design components branding, patterns, textures and colours).

We always use three rational values and three emotional values, but there are eight design components and choices. To add depth and character, designers also consider what the brand stands for and against. What it stands for is incorporated into the 'think' choices, reinforcing the rational aspects of the product. Conversely, what it stands against is integrated into the 'feel' choices, adding emotional resonance and helping to define the product's place in the market.

By carefully balancing these rational and emotional elements, product designers can create items that not only perform their intended utilitarian functions effectively but also forge strong connections with consumers. This holistic design approach ensures that every aspect of the product — from its form and materials to its branding and emotional appeal — works in harmony to tell a cohesive brand narrative and create a compelling user experience.

BRANDING

A brand is as successful as its ability to trigger a feeling of attachment and belonging and, in turn, engender loyalty. It is the delicate process of carefully creating a visual identity, conveying who, what and why a brand is. It is the unique blend of creativity, strategy and skill that establishes a compelling identity that's instantly recognisable in a crowded market, sparking that all-important emotional connection with the audience. Brand design comes in to coordinate deliberate, considered, planned and inventive branding. It is the act of embodying and communicating your brand's personality, from how it sounds, looks and talks, to the values that underpin its actions. It requires a unified system of design elements (such as colour, typography, photography and graphics) to get there.

When we redesigned the branding for the waterproof outdoor accessories company Sealskinz, working with design agency Build, we took it from the notion of a passive seal to a hunting seal, moving it into a Warrior Brand, Role, making it more aggressive and territorial.

Consider FedEx's branding, which means 'We're on it!' When the logo branding design was presented, only one person in the room saw the arrow. The revised FedEx logo has an arrow between the E and the X, signifying, subconsciously, that the delivery service is on the road and closing in on its destination, making us feel assured.

Pattern plays an important role in product design as a visual element that reinforces brand identity and recognition. Louis Vuitton has an iconic monogram canvas, instantly recognisable and synonymous with luxury, brilliance and indulgence. It infers status, signalling durable solidity, travel, experiencing different cultures, class and French luxury. The intertwined L and V are the first symbol, blended nicely to represent the initials of the company, and the second symbol is a design that represents flowers. According to some, George Vuitton, the son of Louis, was inspired by the shadows of the sun as it reflected off Notre Dame's stone finials, creating one of the world's most iconic monograms.

Burberry is another brand for whom pattern is very important, and one I have worked with. Another luxury, aristocratic status symbol, Burberry is renowned for its distinct check pattern, synonymous with the label's heritage and quality craftsmanship. Although it has more recently been subverted by the designer Peter Saville's treatment, it is more than a design, standing for quality and elegance, representative of the brand's commitment to excellence and attitude, and an iconic symbol of British fashion that's recognised worldwide.

TEXTURE

Texture adds another layer of depth to product design. It can convey tactile sensation and create a physical connection with the user, and is very important in terms of making us 'feel.' Patagonia demonstrates this well, where texture has had a tangible and material effect on increasing sales performance. Micro down, a synthetic material used for filling jackets, often fabricated to feel like goose down, transformed the company's fortunes. This revolutionary lightweight insulation provided an unparalleled warmth-to-weight ratio. Similarly, the nubuck suede of a Timberland shoe has the feeling of quality. Texture is crucial, as it connects directly with our senses. Tactility matters.

COLOUR

Finally, in terms of a component that makes us feel, there's colour. It can make us feel a sense of belonging and is hugely influential. It can set the brand tone, influence its image, draw attention and affect emotion, triggering hunger, inspiring trust or eliciting a feeling of calm or excitement. This is why colour should be selected strategically. For example, the colours chosen for the swimwear brand Zoggs (which was the 'child' brand system, alongside 'wonder') was very optimistic. For the United Colors of Benetton, another brand we worked with, the colour palette was designed to make people feel included.

Colour, texture, pattern and brand each contribute a compelling component to the emotional narratives and values that work together to create the company's values or charisma.

If you create a grid that connects 'think' choices to a rational value and 'feel' choices to emotional choices, we can be more certain of designing a product that helps to tell the brand story. It's likely to resonate more effectively in the sub-conscious consumer mind and more likely to be a successful product.

Every choice has a consequence. Each has meaning, whether intended or not. This carries with it responsibility and also privilege, all inherent in brand design. Differing semantic networks and their subjective nature means this can be easy to get wrong. The colour red or blue means different things to different people, but the key question is where the centre of gravity sits.

A design plan that connects product components and product attributes to brand attributes will stand apart much more strongly when scrutinised by the consumer. Along with your brand communication, an integrated approach — with a simple and compelling narrative that makes sense to the truth of the brand — will tell your story. A similar process is used for the communication design stage as well.

BRAND PRACTICE

SALOMON

SALOMON'S XT WINGS TRAIL RUNNING SHOES USED AN ANATOMICAL DESIGN LANGUAGE TO COMMUNICATE THEIR ABILITY TO HANDLE CHALLENGING TERRAINS.

Design Credit: FreshBritain

THE BRAND NEW FUTURE

SALOMON

VISUAL LANGUAGE
INSIDER VIEWPOINT

SALOMON

INSIDER'S LIFE PHOTOGRAPHY
PHOTOGRAPHIC CONTENT:
LIFE INSIGHT OR INSIDER'S VIEWPOINT
PHOTOGRAPHIC DIRECTION:
NATURAL DAYLIGHT, NO FLASH
CREATIVE DIRECTION:
REPORTAGE / DOCUMENTING FACT
STYLING:
NONE

Design Credit: FreshBritain

BRAND PRACTICE

A3 LANDSCAPE DESIGN GRID (DOUBLE PAGE A4)

THE A3 LANDSCAPE (DOUBLE PAGE A4) ADVERTISING GRID IS SET UP AS A FOUR COLUMN GRID ON THE LEFT PAGE & SINGLE COLUMN ON THE RIGHT.

THE ATHLETE/EXPERT TESTIMONIAL IS ALIGNED PRIMARILY WITH THE TOP OR BOTTOM & LEFT MARGINS DEPENDENT ON LEGIBILITY. IF LEGIBILITY IS AN ISSUE THE TESTIMONIAL SHOULD BE PLACED TOP RIGHT OR BOTTOM RIGHT, 12 MM ABOVE THE LOGO.
THE COPY ALWAYS INCLUDES QUOTATION MARKS (" " THE LEFT QUOTATION MARK SHOULD BE SET OUTSIDE THE LEFT EDGE OF THE COPY).
THE TESTIMONIAL COPY SHOULD BE SET ACROSS THREE COLUMNS.
QUOTE COPY: 12 PT.
ATHLETE/EXPERT NAME: 10 PT. (INCLUDE A '-' (HYPHEN) BEFORE NAME)
COPY ALIGNED LEFT OR RIGHT WHEN SET TO THE RIGHT SIDE OF THE LAYOUT.

THE PRODUCT WILL SIT EQUALLY BETWEEN THE TESTIMONIAL & THE PRODUCT NAME, & NOT COVER MORE THAN THREE COLUMNS IN WIDTH OR 90 MM IN HEIGHT.

THE PRODUCT NAME IS LOCATED ABOVE THE PRODUCT & SHOULD SIT APPROXIMATELY 2MM UP FROM THE TOP OF THE PRODUCT IMAGE.
PRODUCT NAME: 10 PT.

THE LOGO WILL SIT DIRECTLY RIGHT ALIGNED ON THE BOTTOM MARGIN, IN 100% BLACK OR 100% WHITE DEPENDENT ON LEGIBILITY.
LOGO SIZE: 50 MM WIDE.

PHOTOGRAPHY & DESIGN CREDITS SIT 1MM BELOW THE BOTTOM MARGIN ON THE LEFT, IN EITHER 100% BLACK OR WHITE COPY DEPENDENT ON LEGIBILITY.
CREDITS COPY: 5 PT.
COPY ALIGNED: LEFT.

THE WEB ADDRESS IS SET HORIZONTALLY IN THE TOP RIGHT OF THE ACTIVITY IMAGE AREA & 100% WHITE COPY IN 100% BLACK BLOCKING. SALOMON SHOULD ALWAYS BE IN INTERSTATE BOLD WITH SPORTS.COM IN INTERSTATE REGULAR FOR LEGIBILITY. THE WEB ADDRESS CAN BE TAILORED TO SPECIFIC ACTIVITIES WHERE NECESSARY. FOR EXAMPLE: SALOMONFREESKI.COM

IN THE EXAMPLE SHOWN, A DOUBLE A4 SPREAD (W: 420MM X H297MM), THE MARGINS ARE TO BE SET AT 10MM, FOR PRESS ADVERTISING* SET THE INSIDE MARGINS AT 15MM TO AVOID INFORMATION LOST IN THE GUTTER. FOR NOTABLY LARGER OR SMALLER SCALE EXECUTIONS THIS GRID SHOULD BE SCALED IN PROPORTION. ALWAYS INCLUDE AT LEAST 3MM OF BLEED.

ALL ADS ARE DESIGNED TO BE RIGHT PAGE OR DPS EXECUTIONS, PLEASE BUY YOUR MEDIA ACCORDINGLY.

*ALWAYS CONSULT SPECIFICATIONS SET BY ADVERTISING PRODUCTION TEAM & ADJUST ACCORDINGLY.

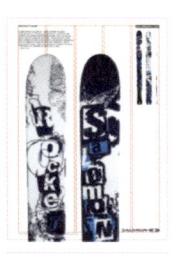

A4 PORTRAIT PRODUCT DESIGN GRID

THE SINGLE PAGE PRODUCT ADVERTISING GRID IS SET UP AS A FIVE COLUMN GRID.
THE PRODUCT IMAGE FILLS FOUR COLUMNS.
360° PRODUCT SHOTS SIT IN THE RIGHT COLUMN & SHOULD NOT TAKE UP MORE THAN ONE COLUMN.

THE ATHLETE/EXPERT TESTIMONIAL IS ALIGNED PRIMARILY WITH THE TOP OR BOTTOM & LEFT MARGINS DEPENDENT ON LEGIBILITY. THE COPY ALWAYS INCLUDES QUOTATION MARKS (" " THE LEFT QUOTATION MARK SHOULD BE SET OUTSIDE THE LEFT EDGE OF THE COPY).
THE TESTIMONIAL COPY SHOULD BE SET ACROSS TWO COLUMNS.
QUOTE COPY: 12 PT.
ATHLETE/EXPERT NAME: 10 PT. (INCLUDE A '-' (HYPHEN) BEFORE NAME)
COPY ALIGNED: LEFT.

THE PRODUCT NAME IS LOCATED 5 MM ABOVE THE TESTIMONIAL.
PRODUCT NAME: 10 PT TYPE.

THE LOGO WILL SIT DIRECTLY RIGHT ALIGNED ON THE BOTTOM MARGIN, IN 100% BLACK.
LOGO SIZE: 50 MM WIDE.

PHOTOGRAPHY & DESIGN CREDITS SIT 1MM BELOW THE BOTTOM MARGIN ON THE LEFT IN 100% BLACK.
CREDITS COPY: 5 PT.
COPY ALIGNED: LEFT.

THE WEB ADDRESS IS SET HORIZONTALLY IN THE TOP RIGHT OF THE LAYOUT & 100% WHITE COPY IN BLACK BLOCKING. SALOMON SHOULD ALWAYS BE IN INTERSTATE BOLD WITH SPORTS.COM IN INTERSTATE REGULAR FOR LEGIBILITY. THE WEB ADDRESS CAN BE TAILORED TO SPECIFIC ACTIVITIES WHERE NECESSARY.
FOR EXAMPLE: SALOMONFREESKI.COM

IN THE EXAMPLE SHOWN, AN A4 SINGLE PAGE (W: 210MM X H297MM), THE MARGINS ARE TO BE SET AT 10MM, FOR PRESS ADVERTISING* SET THE INSIDE MARGIN AT 15MM TO AVOID INFORMATION LOST IN THE GUTTER. FOR NOTABLY LARGER OR SMALLER SCALE EXECUTIONS THIS GRID SHOULD BE SCALED IN PROPORTION. ALWAYS INCLUDE AT LEAST 3MM OF BLEED.

ALL ADS ARE DESIGNED TO BE RIGHT PAGE OR DPS EXECUTIONS, PLEASE BUY YOUR MEDIA ACCORDINGLY.

*ALWAYS CONSULT SPECIFICATIONS SET BY ADVERTISING PRODUCTION TEAM & ADJUST ACCORDINGLY.

4.3 COMMUNICATION
DESIGN

One of the most important teachers in my past, who helped me better understand communication design, was Stephen Male, Art Director at *i-D* magazine. We worked on Levi's and Caterpillar together. Stephen was concerned with how the font and typography, photography and layout of the composition all added up to tell the implicit stories that contribute to the overarching narrative. Our job is to connect these to the brand. In the realm of brand design and communication, the interplay between rational and emotional elements is crucial. As we've touched on, these factors can be categorised into 'think' and 'feel' choices, each serving a distinct purpose in building a connection with the audience.

In brand and communication design terms, this comes down to typography, layout, product imagery and photography and graphics. These elements are instrumental in constructing a rational *I want* connection to the product and brand. They make us contemplate what the brand does and represent the logical aspects of its appeal.

On the other hand, the 'feel' choices are key in fostering an emotional *I need* connection. These include colour, font, imagery and branding elements. They evoke a sense of belonging and operate on a more subconscious level.

Through carefully crafted images, typography and colour schemes, graphic design conveys your brand's essence and values, personality and message, attracting attention and improving memorability.

TYPOGRAPHY

The typography used for Mountain Force, a Swiss-engineered ski company, was all about precision. We chose a typeface that represented that because this was precision apparel from Switzerland — an excellent fit!

If you consider newspapers, the print and typography look at how things are created. *The Times* represents authority. The font Franklin Gothic was invented by the first independent newspaper publisher in America, Benjamin Franklin, one of the country's founding fathers. This represents clarity, progress and being easy to understand.

LAYOUTS

Our layout choice with Inov-8 was designed to make people think this brand *lives on the edge*. We wanted to inspire adventure and step off the beaten track into new territory. Our design layouts, typography and imagery were oriented along the edge of the page, off-screen, bleeding off. It felt like you were being drawn to the edge. A brand where we wanted the layout to look nicely centred and balanced was New Balance. Here, we used Pi, 1.618, the golden ratio, which embodies perfect balance and symmetry. It was first used by Brunelleschi in the Santa Croce's Pazzi Chapel in Florence. A Tuscan creation, as is Italian supercar brand Bizzarrini, where we revisited 1.618 in layouts for the launch, reinforcing the company's Italian cultural roots.

PRODUCT PHOTOGRAPHY

Photo illustration informs and engages the customer, sharing detail about the product and providing information about the values of the brand. It's part of a support system in building interest, understanding and, ultimately, connection with the product. Working with Odlo, a premium outdoor cycling/performance clothing line for active people, a craftsman brand, we chose to show molecular detail in the imagery. This demonstrated commitment to the micro-detail of the brand and its exceptional product design quality. The product photography here leads us to think of microscopic mastery. Likewise, with Leica, the photography shows the detail to demonstrate the precision of German engineering invested in the product, leading us to think of and associate it with engineering mastery.

GRAPHICS

Graphics are used in communication design to convey information, ideas and emotions in a visually compelling and efficient way, to support the shaping of your brand identity. Working with New Balance, we again chose to use the golden ratio, which represents geometry, symmetry and the beauty that exists in nature. It was used because it conveys the kind of balance embodied by New Balance, a strong fit that supports the overall brand ethics. Likewise, with A Bathing Ape, an expensive Japanese streetwear brand, you can see the uncompromising, iconic camo and other graphic elements, emblematic of contemporary street style that resonates self-respect.[16]

Considering the 'feel' choices in communication design, building the emotional *I need* connection is demonstrated through the Levi's red tab in imagery, creating a sense of being original. In Apple, seeing the pulsating light on an iMac or the Apple logo instils a sense of the magical. Nike's swoosh portrays confidence.

Image photography is a powerful tool in communication design. It is a key contributor to making us feel. It can convey authenticity, as seen in the cycling brand Rapha's 'Kings of the Pain' portraits that show grit, determination and the anguish in *you versus the moment*. Or, photography can convey environmental

---

[16] In naming his brand A Bathing Ape, pop-culture obsessed founder Nigo channelled his love for the film *Planet of the Apes* and the Japanese phrase 'A bathing ape in lukewarm water,' a reference to the hyper-consumptive youth who would form the cornerstone of his brand. Source: highsnobiety.com

consciousness, as demonstrated by Patagonia's vast landscape shots featuring diminutive human figures. Here, the company is communicating an enlightened approach: we do not exist to conquer nature but to revere it. These choices in imagery can significantly influence how a brand is perceived and felt by the audience.

Font selection is another critical factor in shaping brand perception. For instance, Arc'teryx uses modern yet elegant serifs to convey a progressive, ego-free feel of leaving no trace. Like nature, it's indelible but ephemeral. Daylesford Organic opts for a welcoming, open font style as a brand centred on nurturing love and bringing you in. These typographic choices contribute significantly to the overall brand personality.

Colour plays a monumental role in brand graphics, evoking specific feelings and associations. Caterpillar's yellow and black colour scheme has become synonymous with outdoor work, while Tiffany's unique blue exudes exclusivity. Coca-Cola, Levi's and Uniqlo use red as a brand colour signifies leadership in the sector.

Warm colours, like red, orange and yellow, tend to evoke feelings of happiness, optimism and energy, while cooler colours, like blue, grey and black, are associated with calmness, mystery, responsibility and elegance.

The magic of brand design lies in the unification and integration of these elements. It's not enough to consider layout, typography or colour in and of themselves. They must be integrated with the company's meaning, strategy and long-term vision to create a cohesive brand expression that works on both the conscious and subconscious levels. Too often, these critical components are considered in isolation and miss the opportunity to be fully integrated.

This integration can be challenging, especially in large businesses where different departments may not communicate effectively. For example, in the automotive sector, on one side you have the interior design of the vehicle and all the considerations around product design that go into the feeling you wish to generate. Meanwhile, on the other side of the company, the car model's manual, advertising and promotion are happening. It's critical that each side be fully aware of the end goal in order to have an integrated brand and product expression. The designer has to be free to deploy their entire bandwidth, delivering a deeper emotional experience around a single choice. But this emotional experience needs to be common across these pieces.

Smaller startups often have an advantage in this regard, as all team members can collaborate closely. For larger enterprises, it's essential to create processes that systematise feelings and thoughts, creating a culture that encourages a unified brand expression.

A real key to successful brand design and communication is ensuring that the emotional experience is consistent across all media used to tell the story, whether it's product design or communication design. This integration of rational and emotional elements, of 'think' and 'feel' choices, is where the true magic of branding exists. It's this holistic approach that ultimately drives growth and success in the marketplace.

MOUNTAIN FORCE

THE TYPOGRAPHY USED FOR MOUNTAIN FORCE, A SWISS-ENGINEERED SKI COMPANY, WAS ALL ABOUT PRÉCISION.

Design Credit: FreshBritain

NEW BALANCE

Photo Credit: Neil Stewart

BRAND PRACTICE

A BRAND WHERE WE WANTED THE LAYOUT TO LOOK NICELY **CENTRED AND BALANCED.**

Life with balance

THE 1050

new balance

Design Credit: FreshBritain

NEW BALANCE

Photo Credit: Neil Stewart

Life with balance

THE 1050

new balance

Design Credit: FreshBritain

4.4 PRODUCT ARCHITECTURE

Product architecture has become increasingly central to brand practice, particularly in the digital age, where online sales dominate and are increasing annually. The structure of a product range serves not only as a means of organisation but also as a navigational tool for consumers browsing on their phones, tablets or laptops. This is exemplified by Netflix's success, which can be attributed in part to superior product architecture that facilitates easy content discovery.

When designing product architecture, brands must focus on fostering both serial and episodic relationships with consumers. A serial relationship encourages people to progress from core products to non-core offerings, thereby increasing revenue per consumer. An episodic relationship, on the other hand, extends this engagement over a longer period.

Effective product architecture should incorporate both image drivers and volume bringers. Image drivers, typically composing 20% of the product range, are high-profile items that capture attention and embody the brand's essence. Volume bringers, making up the remaining 80%, are the more accessible products that generate the bulk of sales. For instance, in the sneaker industry, a premium Air Jordan model might serve as an image driver, while a more affordable Air Force One could be a volume bringer.

The structure of product architecture can vary depending on the brand and industry. Sports brands often organise their products by end use, such as tennis, golf or soccer collections. Other brands may adopt different approaches. Levi's, for example, structure their range based on temporal relevance: Levi's Vintage for the past, Levi's Red Tab for the present and Levi's Made for the future. Fashion brands might organise by product type, as seen with Burberry's outerwear, casual wear and formal wear categories.

Some brands opt for a matrix architecture, combining multiple dimensions. With Dr. Martens, for example, we created a structure based on six consumer types (Provenance, Design, Culture, Value, Quality and Fashion) cross-referenced with product types (1460, Desert Boot, Monkey Boot, 1461). This approach allows for a more nuanced and targeted set of product offerings.

Regardless of the chosen structure, it's essential to ensure that the product architecture facilitates easy navigation, ideally allowing consumers to find desired items within two to three clicks on a mobile device. This needs to be tested. The architecture should also support the development of a visual language and nomenclature that extends from core to non-core products, enabling repetition across seasons and opportunity for economic optimisation.

Brands that fail to develop a robust product architecture risk becoming one-hit wonders, unable to capitalise on initial success. Hunter, known for its Wellington boots, has struggled to expand beyond its weather-dependent core product. In contrast, Lacoste has successfully leveraged its classic polo shirt design to create a thriving footwear line, seamlessly migrating the classic style lines into shoes and demonstrating the importance of translating core propositions into non-core products.

The power of effective product architecture is nicely illustrated by Hollywood super-agent Michael Ovitz, of the Creative Artists Agency (CAA), and his role in the creation of the 1972 film *The Godfather*. Through his earlier talent scout job, Ovitz recognised that the power resided in the talent. Taking a script as the core product and packaging talent around it, he created a successful model for cross-selling and upselling. He would identify a strong script, based on a novel of the same name, and a strong lead actor, and then package unknown actors around this powerful combination. The lead actor he got on board for *The Godfather* was Marlon Brando, around whom he cast an ensemble of relatively unknown actors at the time, including Robert Duvall, Al Pacino and James Caan. He also identified a great score writer who'd worked with Fellini and Visconti to compose the music. Mix in an untested director, Francis Ford Coppola, and you have the famous franchise of *The Godfather*. Rather than take the component parts to the studios, Ovitz took the whole product, packaging everything around the script, and sold it for more than a million dollars. He then went back to the writer and offered a large sum to start writing the next one.

This approach underscores the importance of identifying the script, or core element, within a brand's product architecture, around which other offerings can be built. It is easier to sell many things once than one thing many times.

And so, well-designed product architecture is fundamental to brand success, enabling brands to sell multiple products to consumers over time rather than repeatedly selling a single item. It connects brand meaning to consumer navigation, optimises economic potential and fosters long-term customer relationships.

BRAND PRACTICE

DR. MARTENS

WITH DR. MARTENS, WE CREATED A STRUCTURE BASED ON SIX CONSUMER TYPES CROSS-REFERENCED WITH PRODUCT TYPES.

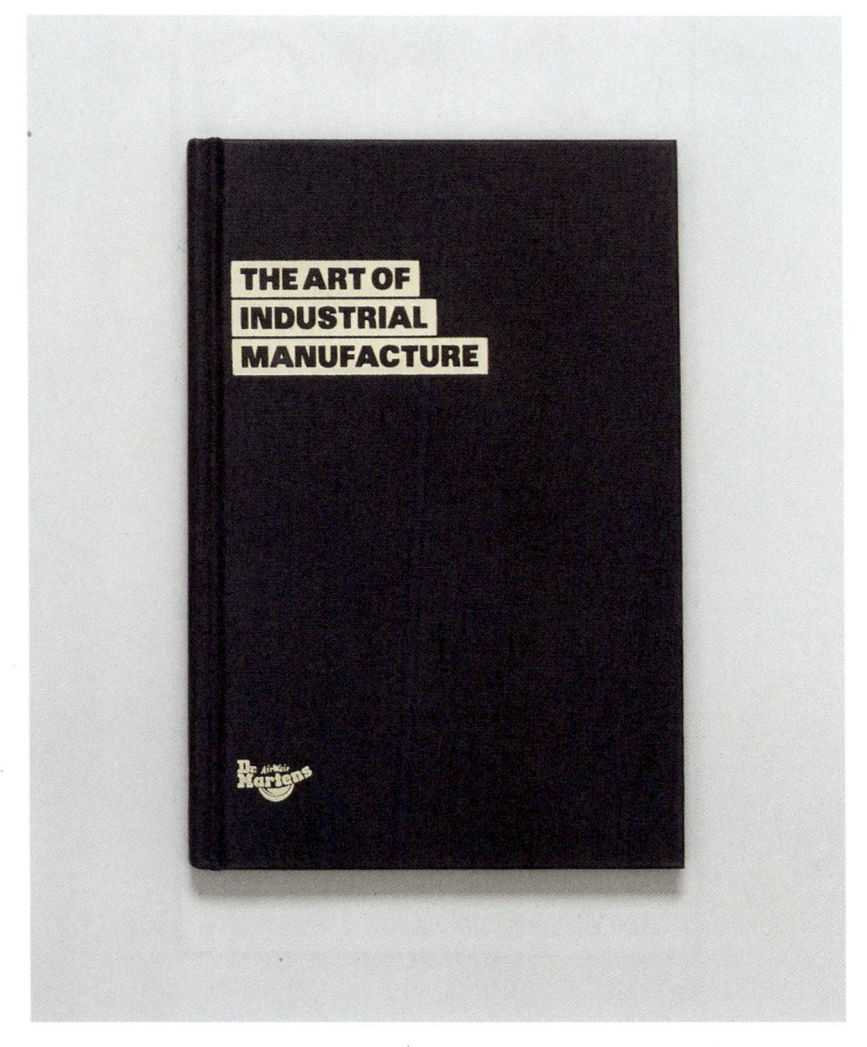

Design Credit: FreshBritain

THE BRAND NEW FUTURE

DR. MARTENS

Photo Credit: Tyrone Lebon

BRAND PRACTICE

Design Credit: FreshBritain

4.5 DIFFUSION OF
INFLUENCE

Understanding the difference between the diffusion of influence and the diffusion of innovation is critical for brands to effectively position themselves in the marketplace and develop successful distribution and influencer strategies. This concept is fundamental to how products and brands spread through the market, typically following a pattern that begins with opinion leaders and progresses through various stages of adoption.

The journey of a brand or product typically starts with opinion leaders — individuals who are early adopters and trendsetters. These could be celebrities, musicians or other cultural icons who are first to embrace a new product when it's at its most exclusive, scarce and expensive. For instance, in the mid-90s, pop stars like Jamiroquai wearing Adidas Gazelle shoes exemplified this, featured in magazines and on our TV screens.

From opinion leaders, the influence diffuses to early adopters, such as journalists, stylists and fashion buyers. These individuals play a crucial role in expanding the product's visibility and volume. They write about it, feature it in stores and contribute to increasing its awareness. This stage sees a slight reduction in price and an expansion in availability.

The early mass market follows, typically comprising fashion-conscious consumers like students and professionals who aspire to emulate the style of cultural icons. At this point, the product starts appearing in wider distribution channels, such as department stores like Harrods or Selfridges, and features in more mainstream publications, like *Vogue*, *Arena FHM* or *Sky Magazine*.

As the product reaches the late market — the general public — its volume increases significantly, often becoming a multi-million-pound seller. The price typically decreases further, and the product may proliferate in terms of colour options or style variations to maximise profits as it flies off the shelves in stores, such as JD Sports. By now, it is pervasively visible: in schools, on the streets, everywhere!

The final phase, which brands generally try to avoid, is the laggard stage. Here, the product may be heavily discounted and sold in discount stores, potentially diluting the brand's prestige.

Understanding this diffusion process allows brands to strategically drive growth through the product life cycle. It helps identify the appropriate distribution channels, media outlets and celebrity ambassadors for each stage. This knowledge is vital for maintaining brand integrity and maximising potential volume.

Successful brands often manage this diffusion process by creating product architectures that cater to different stages of the market. For example, Levi's used different product lines (Vintage, Red Tab, Orange Tab) to target different customer segments. Similarly, at Converse, we used various shoe models to manage the diffusion and maximise growth in each channel: Jack Purcell as our opinion leader, Dr. J in the early mass market, One Star for the mass market and All Star as the late-market product.

It's vitally important for all aspects of a brand's operations — PR, advertising, media buying and sales — to be aligned in understanding and implementing this strategy, with each element fully integrated. The brand's perception is heavily influenced by where it's seen and sold. A seemingly cool brand can quickly lose its appeal if it's distributed through the wrong channels, featured in inappropriate media or seen in the wrong scene.

In essence, the diffusion of influence and innovation provides a framework for brands to strategically manage their growth, maintain their image and maximise their market potential across different consumer segments. It requires a holistic, integrated approach, where all team members understand their role in managing the brand's journey through the marketplace.

4.6 ACTIVATION

The changing communication landscape has made us all journalists. Smartphones and social media have meant that we can broadcast content worldwide at a click of a button. We are all potential (or perhaps de facto) influencers. Brands, too, are increasingly becoming more like media companies, with the challenge of how they can activate in such a way that their message does not simply get lost in the noise.

Brand activation is defined as a marketing strategy that aims to engage consumers through creative, interactive or unexpected elements. It can take many forms, including events, product sampling campaigns, pop-up shops or experiences and interactive digital engagement. All have the same goal: to create a memorable experience and forge a personal connection with the customer. Brand activation is the strategic process of introducing a new brand to the world, with the simple objective of amplifying its presence and stimulating customer action through various channels.

The recent COVID-19 and credit crises, and ongoing cost-of-living and climate-change challenges, are dramatically reshaping the way consumers see their relationship with brands. The shift in recent years has been significant, and brands must understand and respond to their audiences' repositioning and value systems. Now, more than ever, people want ethically sourced, responsibly made, sustainable products. And, along the way, they want to feel valued, treated as unique individuals and part of something larger.

With this dynamic pattern of change, businesses must go back to their central purpose and think in terms of moral imperatives and market purpose, communal alongside commercial gain, and values instead of just value.

We have to reflect, as we activate those sensibilities, because they exist across Gen X, Gen Y and Gen Z, and our consumers are universal. We must be aware of their motivations and the landscapes in which they operate. We also have to be aware of the impact of the influencer and how he or she can help drive awareness and actual material sales. The influencer impact means that we have to build into our activation strategies the ability to co-create products and co-create campaigns. This means that we create versions of them that influencers can select from, giving them the sense of co-creation.

Then, we need to understand that the digital sphere, Web 2.0, is what catalysed brands into effectively being media companies, with rich content and robust social channels. It enabled brands to generate content around which they can design a community to coalesce, which will then drives commerce. Think 'content, community and commerce,' all underpinned by brand-centric narratives. Gen X brands are creating perhaps 50 pieces of content, one a week, but this is tripled for reaching Gen Z, as brands becoming media companies deploy increasingly sophisticated engagement strategies, managed content production and 'owned' social media channels.

Another moving part now on the horizon, with huge unknowns, is the metaverse — a shared virtual reality that allows users to interact and engage with each other. In the metaverse, brands will be invited to explore the opportunity of moving from a physical space to a virtual space, moving from products to actions and from brand effect to brand impact. With the metaverse, the rise of the influencer, shifts in consumer behaviour and the maturation of digital sphere, there will be significant movement and dynamic patterns of change. When brands try to navigate these, and as they activate and grow, there is only one way they can do it.

A child of today will experience more messaging, more inputs, more potential influence and targeting in one year of life than previous generations of humans will have had in an entire lifetime. Faced with the challenge of how to stop being bombarded by all these influences and managing the extent of this dynamic change, as with a child, the answer lies in seeking a true sense of self. It demands identifying and understanding who they are and what they do in order to successfully navigate the rapid change and influence.

It is exactly the same with a brand. When you're looking at the dynamic patterns of consumer change, digital change, influencer change and metaversal change, the only way to understand how to steer through it all and manage this perpetually evolving landscape is to have a true and clear sense of your brand identity. Carving out who you are in your products, your purpose, your personality, your position. Having a critical sense of those four things is what enables brands to make the right choices when faced with these critical and continuous elements of change.

This is the key to how brands should activate and how they can grow.

As we've suggested, every brand and every person now has the potential to be a media company, which is why we have seen the rise of the personal brand. Having a true sense of self will help us work our way through the noise. That sense of self will act as your compass and guide you in the right direction at all times.

We so often see brands rushing to embrace the next new thing, whether that is Twitter, TikTok or the use of influencers. We're all trying to jump onto the latest trend and stay ahead of the curve. Through it all, it always comes back to great storytelling and knowing who you are, knowing what you're selling and knowing what effect you want to have on the people you interact with. Sometimes, not doing something is an active choice. Waiting to see, not rushing into things and letting things play out can be a wise strategy.

Consider the clothes we wear. I am always struck by the changes in fashion, colour, shapes, cuts, influencer trends, cultural changes. Our clothes are subject to so much change. Yet when I look at my clothes, they'd be recognisable to my grandparents and my grandparents' parents. For the most part, trousers haven't changed, jumpers haven't changed, shirts haven't really changed. There are the fundamentals — the material, the construction — that are consistent, regardless of the latest trends. Understanding what changes and what doesn't change is important in both product terms and communication terms.

The media will continue to change, but the stories we tell through those channels will continue to be stories that exist in our subconscious, stories that we've heard through the ages and that our ancestors have passed on.

These narratives don't change. They are consistent around the world, because our human emotions are universal. We all feel happiness; we all feel sadness. We all relate to the same push and pull. For the most part these days, we wear similar clothing. At times, when the world seems so overwhelming, it's worth looking deeper and seeing that, actually, there's a lot that's stable and familiar. Stories and storytelling as critical components of growth don't really change that much.

Other things that change very little are the moments when we are reminded of our mother.

"TO ME, SELLING LEVI'S IS SYNONYMOUS WITH MY MUM"

MUM

MOMENTS

MADRESFIELD COURT

"Remember, you're no better than anybody else, and anybody else isn't better than you."

That would be something my mum would say to me as we drove to work at John Street Market to sell our wares. Nestled between Lumb Lane and Manningham Lane, in the infamous red light district of Bradford, we served an unimaginable community of characters from the underbelly of the town.

Working on the Madresfield Court brand with John and Lucy Chenevix-Trench, we helped rethink their estate as a brand.

It has been in the same family for 29 generations, where Evelyn Waugh wrote Brideshead Revisited and where Elgar's father tuned the pianos. Working with John and Lucy, on one of Britain's oldest and most esteemed brands, was a wonderful time and a true privilege.

Driving up the drive, I'd think of my mum driving me to the markets and saying that nobody was better than anyone else.

It was and always will be 'a mum moment.'

LEVI'S

As recounted earlier, we would buy half-ton bales of denim from a distribution depot in Huddersfield and sort them into brand types. The terrible brands we used to sell with my mother in Leeds Market, Halifax Market and Dewsbury Market. The Levi's, the real value in those bales, we'd take to London to sell at Camden Market.

To me, selling Levi's is synonymous with my mum.

Years later, I had a serious snowboard accident that led to reconstructive surgery on my shoulder, which created a pulmonary embolism that nearly killed me. I had to spend a year giving myself injections and blood thinners to make sure that I didn't have a recurrence of the embolism. I also couldn't travel anywhere because of the risk of a blood clot dislodging and fatally blocking my lung arteries.

So when I got the call to come and un-fuck Levi's, I had to explain that they had to come to me.

They did, and in London, we spent three days redesigning the brand that had paid for my education, but also the brand I used to sell in the markets with my mum.

When the leadership team of Levi's walked into my London office, that was 'a mum moment.'

5. THE FUTURE OF EVERYTHING

In this chapter, we confront the urgent environmental and societal challenges that define our present moment and will shape our future. We consider why this particular point in history demands our immediate attention. We also look at why Gen Z stands at the forefront of this juncture relative to the existential environmental crisis we're facing.

This chapter goes beyond identifying the problem and considers what can be done about it, both for brands seeking to make a meaningful impact and we as individuals and consumers hoping to contribute to positive change. Through this examination, we also uncover reasons for hope in the face of daunting challenges.

The impact of climate change is far reaching, pressing and becoming ever-more severe. The urgency of our world's situation has never been clearer: temperatures are reaching unprecedented heights, droughts and flooding have become increasingly devastating, and weather patterns have grown exceptionally extreme. Hurricanes and similar weather events are pounding us with previously unseen ferocity, while our planet's natural cooling systems—ice packs, glaciers and sea ice—are diminishing at an alarming rate. This degradation of the Earth's regulatory systems isn't just a weather concern—it's a cascade that threatens to amplify pollution, accelerate species extinction and ultimately exacerbate human suffering through increased starvation, poverty and forced migration.

SO WHY FRESHBRITAIN?

Over the last 25 years, FreshBritain have been fortunate to work with some of the world's pre-eminent outdoor brands, including Nike ACG, Salomon, Arc'teryx, Jack Wolfskin, Kjus, Odlo, Montane, Mountain Hardware and Simond. We have seen how they've struggled with the different dynamic changes to their environment. The mountain, similar to the ocean, is a proverbial canary in the coal mine, providing early warning of the danger. We've seen how climate change has affected people and businesses and, in turn, how it has affected our own business. There is self-interest here, too. We need to consider what the future of everything is and, in doing so, what is the future of growth.

THE EVOLUTION OF SUSTAINABLE BRAND GROWTH: A NEW PARADIGM

In today's business landscape, two crucial questions emerge at the intersection of branding and sustainability: how can we grow brands in a more sustainable way, and how can we design them to achieve ongoing growth more sustainably? To address these questions, we must first understand the conventional mechanisms of brand growth and then explore how these can be adapted for a more sustainable future.

As set out in earlier chapters, the tried and tested FreshBritain formula for brand growth is composed of three fundamental elements: Positioning, Personality and Purpose. When these align effectively, they create a powerful engine for sustainable growth. Strong brand design combined with clear positioning attracts customers and generates turnover. The key is then maintaining this relationship, creating an episodic and serial connection with consumers that drives profitability. When further enhanced by emotional engagement through clear brand purpose, this can significantly boost enterprise value.

CASE STUDIES IN TRANSFORMATIVE BRAND GROWTH

Several notable examples of brands that we have worked with illustrate the power of this approach:

Salomon: The Power of Innovation-Led Positioning

Salomon's transformation demonstrates how proper positioning can drive substantial growth. In 2007, we worked with the company to redesign their value proposition. As set out earlier, we delved into their vast patent portfolio of over 8,000 mountain sports innovation patents, enabling us to reposition the brand as 'The Mountain Sports Company.' This clear positioning led to strategic choices, including the successful venture into trail running, helping drive revenue from $300 million to more than $1 billion.

Arc'teryx: Emotional Connection Through Brand Personality

Arc'teryx's success story revolves around creating a compelling and addictive brand personality centred on living in harmony with nature. This positioning, contrasted with competitors' more aggressive approaches, led to threefold profit growth by establishing deep emotional connections with consumers who shared their values.

Volvo Defense: Purpose-Driven Enterprise Value

The rebranding of Volvo Defense into Arquus illustrates the power of purpose-driven repositioning. We worked on getting the mission and purpose right, centred on mobility defence systems. We looked back at the long history of warfare, the original military defence system (the horse, Equus in Latin), and Arquus, blacksmith of the gods, making weapons and armour. As described earlier, evolving from a diesel truck manufacturer to an innovator of mobile defence systems brought 72% year-on-year growth and increased the company's enterprise value by $200 million through an improved market multiple. Today, they are literally taking the fight to Putin.

Dr. Martens: The Integration Success Story
Perhaps the most compelling example is Dr. Martens, where the integration of Positioning, Personality and Purpose around 'rebellious self-expression' transformed a declining £90 million revenue business into a £3.5 billion flotation in 11 years.

THE ECONOMIC IMPACT OF BRAND VALUE

What's often overlooked is the significant contribution of brand value to company market capitalisation. This can be up to 20% for most companies and can increase to 40% for service companies. This understanding becomes even more crucial when we consider that economies are essentially the sum of their brands, as all goods and services carry brand identity to some degree. By extension, understanding the value-add to economies of our brands and how to maximise and grow brand value is a critical strategy for economic prosperity, where assets from both physical and non-physical sources significantly influence a nation's economy.

MY DAMASCENE CONVERSION

After 25 years and 250 brand designs, we started to have a series of realisations and experience our own directional change of heart. We've begun to reflect on what we do and question our role in the sustainability conversation. We asked ourselves, *"Have we just helped people make more and sell more?"* And, *"Where is all that stuff now?"* How can we look at what we do and change what we do? How can we help brands grow more positively and more sustainably? We in the branding business have arrived at a critical moment of reflection. The challenge now is to evolve from simply helping companies sell more to considering the long-term impact of these activities. This raises important questions about the life cycle of products and the responsibility of brand designers in promoting more sustainable growth patterns. It is the dawning sustainability imperative.

LOOKING FORWARD

The future of brand growth lies in finding ways to align commercial success with sustainable practices. This requires a fundamental shift in how we approach brand design and development, ensuring that growth strategies consider not just immediate commercial gains but long-term environmental and social impact. The challenge for brand designers and strategists is to help companies achieve their growth objectives while contributing positively to a more sustainable future.

5.1 A HISTORY OF BRAND COMMUNICATIONS

As we have outlined, the evolution of brand communication reflects the broader changes in societal communication. In the 1950s, brand communication was primarily product-focused, presenting items in a rational manner, and was just about selling more products. This approach evolved into brand advertising in the 1960s and '70s, which began to emotionalise brand propositions, encouraging consumers to buy products based on brand identity rather than just functionality.

The 1980s and '90s saw a shift towards more persuasive communication techniques. With the rise of the internet and social media, brand communication further evolved into community-based strategies, aiming to generate both community engagement and commerce. We now see a more engaged consumer, understanding and flexing their personal agency. In recent years, there has been a movement towards impactful communication, exemplified by companies like Patagonia, which, as we've said, has pledged its profits to an Earth trust and declared the planet their sole shareholder.

This evolution becomes starkly apparent when examining historical advertisements, such as that 1950 cigarette ad featuring

Reagan. This raises questions about how future generations might judge us, how history will consider our current brand communications, especially in the context of global challenges like climate change. We need to address the tough questions and look at how we can do better. We need to address the new proposition: How can we grow while at the same time making less stuff?

While many companies still rely on traditional brand advertising and persuasive communication, there's a growing need for more impactful and responsible messaging. This shift is driven by changing consumer expectations, particularly among younger people, who are more concerned with sustainability, social responsibility and meaningful personal identity.

5.2 A NEW FORM OF GROWTH (GENERATIONS DRIVING CHANGE)

Part of the solution is exploring how we can grow, educate and design enterprises and brands more sustainably. This comes into focus when we think about managing global population growth, as we move from 7 billion people on the planet to 12 billion by the end of the century. We need to work out how we move production towards 'zero' and move consumption 'beyond zero,' while using the knowledge, intelligence and experience that resides within a brand to move the brand to 'zero' as well. To do this, we must reimage the future of brands. The concept of growth is central to this evolution. Traditional growth models, which are socially obsessive and economically compulsive, are increasingly seen as ecologically regressive. We must move away from these traditional 'bad growth' values, where our individual growth status is measured by the square-footage of our holiday home and the chunkiness of our wristwatch. Business and commercial metric drivers are based on revenue growth, profit growth and market share. All plumb down untrammelled growth, accentuating the notion of growth being economically compulsive. And as we've noted, almost half the world's population went to the polls in 2024, having been sold promises of economic growth, without which politicians' other policy pledges (and their survival in office) won't come to pass.

There's a pressing need to reimagine growth in a way that's sustainable and responsible. This 'good growth' is described in the concept of doughnut economics, an economic model that aims to help humanity thrive in the 21st century by meeting the needs of all people while protecting the environment. It envisions an alternative economic system where the positioning becomes simple: The sweet spot is where growth has to thrive above the economic threshold for purposeful, sustainable life but below the ecological threshold for unsustainable life and environmental destruction.

Understanding generational shifts is crucial for brand evolution. We've covered how Gen X was motivated by status and accumulation of possessions, Gen Y shifted towards community and the accumulation of content, and digital-native Gen Z is more focused on self-identity and accumulation of experiences, driven by values. Young people face unique challenges, including information overload, unreliable truths, overstimulation, multiple crises, eco-anxiety and unprecedented self-obsession fuelled by social media. The brilliant design, innovation and creative strategist Roddy Darcy observes that Gen Z are redefining our perspectives around purpose, how we live our lives, the rules we live by and how we spend our time. Slowly, we see consumers being less defined by what they own and more defined by what they do.

5.3 BUT WHY GEN Z?

Why is it important to design our brands for the 11- to 26-year-old Gen Zers?
1. They are the pioneers who are driving purpose.
2. They're change seekers, challenging the rules by which we live.
3. They're the reductionists who will change how we live.
4. They are the guardians who will save us time.

For brands to remain relevant and successful, they must adapt to these changing dynamics, particularly those affecting Gen Z. This generation is set to become the world's largest economic group by 2040, making their perspectives and values crucial for future brand strategies. In the next three years, there will be more people who live on Earth who were born in the 21st century than were born in the 20th century. The argument becomes a simple one: If we want to future-proof our commerce, brands and economies, we have to shift them around the motivations of this empowering generation. Gen Z lives 'beyond zero,' and so we need to learn how to design brands to live (and thrive) at net zero and beyond.

Brands must move beyond traditional growth models and focus on impactful, sustainable communication that resonates with the values and concerns of younger generations.

The future of brand communication lies in understanding and addressing these evolving consumer motivations, particularly the shift from defining oneself by possessions to being defined by actions and impact. Companies must strive to align with the values of sustainability, social responsibility and personal identity, which are increasingly important to consumers. This evolution is not just about doing the right thing ethically; it's a necessary adaptation for brands to remain commercially viable in a changing world.

5.4 CORPORATE PROTOCOLS

We've got to start redesigning our institutions and companies with the following aspirational goals in mind:
1. We put beliefs at the heart of strategy.
2. We create strategies that put people first, positioning them at the top rather than organising top-down.
3. We look at mutuality as well as singularity.
4. We redefine conventional metrics as impacts.
5. We imagine the external effect of all our internal decisions.
6. We consider 'what if' instead of just 'what is.'
7. We look at efficiency as the enemy of diversity.

5.5 BRAND PROTOCOLS

We have to start redesigning our brands with the following in mind:

8. We reimagine the brand as the experience.
9. We look at intellectual property (IP) and try to open source it as public property, helping people to be defined by what they know over what they have.
10. We redefine storytelling as story-doing.
11. We start to look at brands and how we can save people's time rather than waste time with never-ending content churn.
12. We redesign 'lifestyle' as 'purposeful life.'
13. We look at a simple declaration of brand beliefs rather than perpetual brand outreach.
14. We regard the digital sphere and the physical sphere as a single entity.

5.6 PRODUCT PROTOCOLS

We must begin to redesign our products with the following in mind:

15. We look at the product as the byproducts.
16. We look at fixed solutions and start to reimagine them as circular and fluid.
17. We reimagine regenerative sourcing and manufacturing.
18. We design products with high functional life expectancy. But if they last 20 years, you still want to wear them and use them, so they must have a high aesthetic life expectancy. That suggests massive changes for the principles of fashion and product design.
19. We design products with multi-use afterlives.
20. We look at knowledge, experience and intelligence as platforms within brands that can become channels for future growth.

These are 20 protocols to redesign brands onto a pathway towards zero energy consumption.

5.7 THE THREE BIG CS: COVID-19, CLIMATE AND CONFLICT

A trio of big-picture issues that have adversely affected our lives in recent years — COVID-19, climate and conflict — are truly global, highlighting the disconnect between universal challenges and our existing governance structures. We, as citizens of the world, have very few democratic levers to pull. These crises ignore our national borders, yet our primary governance mechanisms remain largely confined within those borders. The world is made up of 195 countries, each with a leader, cabinet, parliament or process for managing its people, and the domestic repercussions of these global issues make clear the magnitude of the challenge.

Where is our voice in wanting to decide who manages pandemics globally, or climate globally, or conflict globally? The closest we have to global governance is international organisations like the United Nations, the World Health Organization and various treaty organisations. However, these bodies have limited power and often rely on voluntary cooperation from member states. Our leverage is limited, reduced to influencing global issues by electing leaders who prioritise cooperation and multilateral solutions, through civil society organisations and via non-governmental agencies that advocate for global issues. We are, therefore, limited to the choices we make through consumerism — and how we spend our money.

We can, in fact, wield power by making sustainable choices and supporting companies with upstanding global practices. We've already seen movement towards buying brands that represent the future we want to see. Moving forward, more of us will buy goods and services from brands that shape the future we want to live in, and support brands that symbolise the future we want to be. We will vote with our wallets. We should buy the future we want to see!

Considering it in this way, we start to see how important and influential brands can be in terms of creating the space — and the mandate — for our global leadership to follow.

We must begin to reimagine how we generate growth without making more products, and that seems like the most unnatural and impossible thing. How on earth can we grow while we're making less stuff?

Well, it's already happening!

5.8 MAKING MORE
WITH LESS

The music industry provides a compelling example of how businesses can adapt and thrive by shifting from selling products to selling experiences. Two decades ago, major labels, like Columbia Records in New York, focused primarily on selling compact discs. According to Luminate data, some 650 million music CDs were sold in the US alone in 2005. The company's business model revolved around producing physical albums, with tours serving as a promotional tool to drive record sales. However, the advent of digital music platforms like Napster and iTunes completely disrupted this model, forcing the industry to pivot.

As CD sales plummeted, the industry had to reinvent itself by focusing on what was once a byproduct: live performances. Today, we see artists like Taylor Swift, ABBA, Adele and even geriatric rockers like the Rolling Stones are generating astronomical revenues from concert performances, far surpassing what they could have earned from CD sales in the past. This shift has not only helped the industry survive but has put it in a stronger economic position by selling experiences and memories rather than physical products that wind up in the trash. This is significant, as the US Environmental Protection Agency says it will take centuries for a plastic CD to completely decompose in landfill. Centuries.

This transformation in the music industry sets a precedent for other sectors, particularly the outdoor industry. Simond, the mountaineering brand we've talked about, exemplifies this shift. We worked to redesign the outdoor brand, aiming to help them grow 35-fold over a five-year period. This exponential growth is occurring while Simond reduces its environmental impact, reimagining its business model and moving towards a regenerative, beyond-zero platform.

The transformation strategy will involve leveraging its knowledge, intelligence and experience in mountaineering to create growth platforms that don't rely solely on producing physical goods. Instead, the company will explore expansion into areas such as instruction, skills development, fitness, qualifications, examinations, educational platforms, guiding expeditions and expedition preparation.

These new growth avenues could now include coaching, well-being services, repair services, second-hand sales, rental programmes, physiotherapy, nutrition advice, travel services, insurance and tour hosting. All of these pursuits generate revenue without necessarily increasing product manufacturing or contributing to landfill waste.

"I WAS ONLY SEVEN OR EIGHT, BUT WAS STRUCK BY THESE NEW BRANDS THAT MY DAD KNEW BUT I'D NEVER SEEN BEFORE."

DAD

MOMENTS

BURBERRY

Experiences are often at their most potent when they remind us of those we love and miss.

When I was at school, my dad worked away in Worcester, where he was the Buying Director of Great Universal Stores. GUS, as it was known at the time, had a stable of house brands that used to report into my dad. One of which was Burberry.

Back then, Burberry was a little more than a few pages of overcoats in the GUS catalogue.

It was my father who arranged a collaboration with Jaguar, where an XJ8 was upholstered in the Burberry check.

Clearly an important step in the collaboration universe to come.

A few years ago, we were invited to help redesign Burberry. When we met the team in London, not long after my father had passed away, it was with a huge dose of nostalgia and pride that I was able to tell the leadership team that the Burberry-checked XJ8 was my dad's work.

It was an emotional 'dad moment.'

CALVIN KLEIN

When I was 21, my father took my brother and me on a trip to New York City. Through his work, he knew people in the garment district, and we went to a number of offices, where we were made to feel very welcome.

As a young lad from Halifax who had barely travelled outside of the UK, it was amazing to be in New York but also unbelievable that people in New York knew my dad. This was definitely an eye-opener for me — that there was a bigger world out there — and I wanted to be part of it.

Before his death, my dad suffered from dementia, and just before the start of the COVID-19 pandemic, I was invited to go and pitch in New York for the redesign of the Calvin Klein brand.

I knew my dad was close to the end of his life when I entered the lift in the Calvin Klein headquarters. And I knew he would be filled with pride that his son would be holding court in a boardroom in Manhattan's garment district, just as he had done 30 years before.

COVID-19 happened, and the project never went ahead, but it was a true 'dad moment' nonetheless.

LVMH

As a young boy, we would travel by car to France, to Normandy, where we would enjoy camping holidays. While there, we would take a trip to Deauville and watch the rich Parisians take in the boardwalk air.

My dad loved to people watch and would point out the various brands people were wearing: Lacoste, Chanel, Fila, Louis Vuitton.

I was only seven or eight, but I was struck by these new brands that my dad knew but I'd never seen before.

Decades later, I was invited to LVMH House in London to present my thinking on brands to the company's leaders.

The room was full of people who had graduated from Harvard, grandes écoles, the Sorbonne and Oxbridge, and it was present in my mind that I had not.

As I stood up to make my 20-minute presentation, my computer failed, and the carefully crafted images on the screen went dead. The audience looked at me in anticipation, and I didn't know what to say. I had to think of a way to give myself the time to think of what to say, and then I noticed that the 30 or so people in front of me each had a pen and paper. Having no choice, I improvised.

"You are the future leaders of the world's largest luxury brand group," I said. *"Can you answer, in one word, this question?"*

I let the silence hang in the air for a moment.

"What," I asked, *"is a brand?"*

The idea was that this would give me another minute to figure out what to say, but I was still grappling with the ramifications of no computer, no presentation, a big opportunity tragically lost. After a minute went by, I still didn't know what to say, so I decided to walk around the room, pick up each piece of paper and read out the answers.

As I read their responses, I realised something extraordinary. Each answer was different. They'd given me 30 different answers to the question, 'What is a brand?'

I neatly stacked the papers, slowly scanned their faces and told them, *"You are the 30 future leaders of the world's leading luxury brands group. I asked you a simple question — what is a brand? — to which you've given me 30 different answers. That's a problem. If you need help with this problem, this is my phone number. Thank you for your time today."*

I wrote my number on the pad, left it there on the desk and left the room.

As I walked out, I remembered my dad in Deauville, telling little-boy me about those luxury brands. In retrospect, this was the daddy of all 'dad moments.'

THE BRAND NEW FUTURE

ARC'TERYX

Design Credit: FreshBritain

THE FUTURE OF EVERYTHING

CREATING A COMPELLING AND ADDICTIVE BRAND PERSONALITY CENTRED ON LIVING IN HARMONY WITH NATURE.

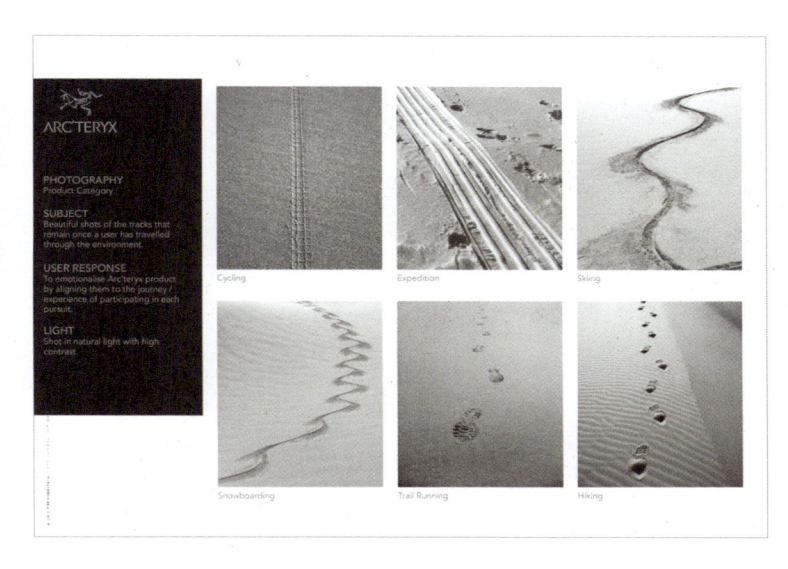

ARC'TERYX

Design Credit: FreshBritain

THE FUTURE OF EVERYTHING

183

ARC'TERYX

Design Credit: FreshBritain

THE FUTURE OF EVERYTHING

6. GROWTH IN PERPETUITY (IN THEORY)

Here, as a gateway into the notion of growth in perpetuity, we will take a rather deep dive into regenerative thinking theory.

Designer and consultant Josie Warden puts this best in her 'What does regenerative thinking mean?' article for the Royal Society of Arts. She asserted that a regenerative mindset *"is one that sees the world as built around reciprocal and co-evolutionary relationships, where humans, other living beings and ecosystems rely on one another for health, and shape (and are shaped by) their connections with one another."*[17]

In this chapter, we'll take Josie's regenerative insight and translate it into regenerative brand thinking.

Brands are living through an unprecedented period of dramatic change:
- The world of work is changing.
- Biodiversity is declining.
- Identity is flexing.
- Politics is being redrawn.
- Societal norms are shifting.
- Climate change is biting.

There is growing awareness that incremental changes to existing thinking and actions may not be sufficient to address such upheaval. Instead, these disruptions could pave the way for more significant, regenerative changes to brands.

---

[17] What does 'regenerative' thinking mean? Josie Warden, Royal Society of Arts, 2021.
Source: thersa.org/rsa-journal/2021/issue-4/feature/what-does-regenerative-thinking-mean

Instead of existing in architectures within which all the brand creativity is fixed, in order to meet the challenges of the future, brands will become more fluid. The creativity of others will be included and inspired, and creativity will grow. We will see a shift away from the more traditional brand architecture towards a 'brand garden' concept. Brand gardens are purpose-built, future-proofed marketing ecosystems, owned and operated by individual brands in partnership with an independent technology partner.

6.1 BRANDS — A LIVING SYSTEM PERSPECTIVE

Thinking about brands as living systems offers a fresh perspective that can help them thrive in a changing, increasingly complex world. This approach views brands as dynamic, interconnected entities embedded within larger ecosystems, constantly adapting, evolving and innovating. Here are some of the new living-systems form and function types we will see:

1. *Nested:* At the core of this perspective is the concept of nested systems, where regenerative systems sit within, are affected by and affect other systems. Brands don't exist in isolation; they are part of larger economic, social and environmental systems, both influencing and being influenced by them. This interconnectedness means that brands must be aware of their place within these broader contexts and understand how their actions ripple through various layers of the ecosystem.
2. *Living:* This reflects the living nature of brands and their constant movement between states of convergence, divergence and emergence. Too much convergence can lead to rigidity, stifling innovation and adaptability. Conversely, excessive divergence may result in chaos and a lack of coherent identity. The key to resilience lies in maintaining a balance, allowing for ongoing adaptability in response to changing conditions.

3. *Emergent:* As brands interact with various nested systems, new properties and innovations can arise in unpredictable, non-linear ways. This emphasises the importance of responsiveness over rigid analysis, as brands must be prepared to adapt quickly to unforeseen developments and opportunities.
4. *Diversity:* Efficiency drives will become the enemy of diversity. While efficiency-driven approaches often seek singularity and streamlined processes, a regenerative perspective recognises the value of diversity. Abundance and the proliferation of ideas, approaches and offerings can lead to more resilient and adaptive brand ecosystems.
5. *Mutuality (and reciprocity):* These are fundamental to living systems, including brands. Relationships that create mutual net benefits emerge from bidirectional exchanges rooted in abundance and generosity. This shift towards mutually beneficial interactions can foster stronger, more sustainable connections between brands and their stakeholders.

For brands to thrive in this context, they must integrate regenerative thinking into their core principles today, to enable regenerative actions tomorrow. This requires a fundamental shift in how we perceive brands and their role in the world. Our beliefs about how the world works and how brands fit within it will guide our actions and strategies.

THE CHALLENGE FOR BRANDS

In this interconnected landscape, relationships and interdependencies have never been so important. Brands must recognise that they are part of complex, emergent systems that defy linear prediction. By adopting a regenerative perspective, they can better navigate this unpredictable terrain and foster resilience, innovation and sustainable growth in an ever-changing world. Integrating regenerative actions tomorrow depends on the regenerative thinking we design into brands today. Underpinning our brand systems are our beliefs about how our world works and how our brands fit within them — this will guide our actions. A regenerative perspective can help brands thrive in this evolving landscape.

6.2 REGENERATIVE BRAND THINKING

We have seen that regenerative brand thinking is a mindset that aims to restore, preserve and improve the health of our natural environment and society. It's a more ambitious approach than sustainability and is based on what we have evidenced. It's the idea that businesses can be active agents of positive change. We have seen the shift in consumer expectations for brands to take responsibility for the environment. According to consultancy Human8, 85% of people globally believe brands should help protect the future of the planet, and 78% believe we need to go beyond just *sustaining* the planet.[18]

Brands need to consider:

Place: Instead of top-down solutions, look at the potential of 'place-up' contextually centred solutions.

Value: Instead of the metric being financial value, consider impacts, consequences and contribution, with greater focus on knowledge, skills, intelligence, culture, behaviour and infrastructure.

Flow: Instead of fixing knowledge, consider how it can be designed to flow with circularity across and between layers, helping the system to regenerate. Think about working in the open to help others engage and influence.

---

[18] Empowering brands for a regenerative tomorrow, Camille Nicita (22 Feb 2024).
Source: www.wearehuman8.com/blog/empowering-brands-for-aregenerative-tomorrow/

'I': Instead of focusing on your outer state, consider starting with your inner conditions — how you think, reflect and communicate. Designing regeneratively involves some developmental aspects, and requires us to work on ourselves.

Vision: Instead of starting with 'What is,' consider asking 'What if?', building a hopeful, long-term vision for your brand's future.

Perspective: Instead of singular perspectives, consider differences and different perspectives. Where are the blind spots, and how might they be illuminated?

People: Instead of focusing on singular solutions, consider how the mutuality and reciprocity of people can build shared ownership solutions using a vision project as a catalyst, not an end point.

From here, and with a new perspective that transforms our approach migrating from brand architects towards brand gardeners, we can start to turn philosophy into practice via protocols.

6.3 REGENERATIVE CORPORATE PROTOCOLS

Corporate protocols should:
1. *Reimagine Beliefs as Strategy*
   - Define the brand beliefs — what it stands for and against.
   - This informs the brand's moral purpose, along with the market purpose.
   - Incorporate these beliefs into the corporate growth strategy and integrate positive impact as a measured output.
2. *Reimagine 'Top-Down' as 'People-Up'*
   - Look beyond traditional top-down hierarchies that can be reductive and restrictive.
   - Instead, consider people and 'place-up' solutions. Encouraging more cognitive diversity and contextual meaning will enrich and enliven thinking.

- Continuously inspire and encourage innovative thinking from an organic, connected and empowered network.
3. *Reimagine Singularity as Mutuality*
    - Instead of focusing on singular solutions, consider how mutuality and reciprocity of people can build cultures and shared ownership solutions.
    - Relationships should be open and fluid, rather than one-way and closed.
    - This will unlock collective gain, with the mutual sharing of ideas for shared benefit becoming a cultural tailwind.
4. *Reimagine Metrics as Impacts*
    - To drive real change and deliver real positive impact, corporations must look beyond traditional metrics of success, such as market share, revenue and profit growth.
    - Consider yardsticks of success based on wider impacts, such as community engagement, cultural enrichment, education or environmental consequences.
    - Re-engineering metrics of success at the corporate C-Suite level will positively drive impact initiatives throughout an organisation. The 'what' of every working day will be catalysed by the individual and communal 'why.'
5. *Reimagine Internal as External*
    - Instead of always focusing on the 'outer' and external actions, reflect on personal internal position and conditions.
    - Ask internally what you can do better, and accept 'We don't know everything.'
    - Acting regeneratively can turn what we don't know into a superpower, if we involve self-awareness and self-development before acting and articulating externally.

6. *Reimagine 'What is' as 'What if'*
   - Think big, with a bigger and bolder vision that delivers a positive impact.
   - Move beyond accepting the world as it is, and reimagine it with regenerative outcomes.
   - Deploy a courageous and inspiring vision to challenge orthodoxy, and act as a catalyst for a more hopeful future. Aim for bright, far-off stars that will bring previously unreachable moons into your orbit.
7. *Reimagine Efficiency as Diversity*
   - Reductionism seeks singularity and efficiency in the pursuit of mass-produced scale, but efficiency is the enemy of diversity, proliferation and abundance.
   - Rather than investing in the perceived efficiency of relentless leadership, invest in the potential of fearless teamship, listening to and taking diverse viewpoints in the pursuit of a greater collective solution.
   - Instead of singular perspectives, exploring different perspectives will reveal as-yet unseen opportunities.

6.4 REGENERATIVE BRAND PROTOCOLS

1. *Reimagine The Brand as The Experience*
   - Brands can elevate beyond a singular focus on product creation and transaction, to encompass wider brand experiences that will have much less negative impact on people and the planet.
   - The brand and its meaning system becomes a wider platform for diverse consumer interactions.
   - The brand can be a catalysing force for positive impact within their wider ecosystem, extending engagement beyond a singular product-focused transaction.

2. **Reimagine Intellectual Property as Public Property**
   - Reconsider what of the brand's IP has traditionally been protected for competitive advantage, but could be put to communal advantage if open sourced as public property.
   - Consider all the experience and intelligence that resides within an organisation for product advantage and how it can be deployed for wider benefit and positive impact.
   - Assess what can be made open source with other organisations to share for mutual innovation. Imagine IP unleashed as Influential Purpose.
3. **Reimagine Storytelling as Story-Doing**
   - Brands can state a declaration of their beliefs, but rather than create brand meaning with synthetic advertising through storytelling, it's possible to re-allocate advertising resources towards story-doing initiatives for positive impact.
   - This means redeploying ad spend to impact-driven strategies, rather than adding to the noise of brand clutter and communication.
   - Brands can still tell stories, but now from within the context of story-doing. Think of orienting consumer aspiration towards collective impact, versus just the impact on me.
4. **Reimagine Time Saved as Time Experienced**
   - Brands have sought to dominate consumers' time to drive consumption but must now give more time for positive consumer experiences.
   - This means abdicating brand engagement to individual consumer choice.
   - This will help move people from digital-dependent time to more time spent living.

5. *Reimagine Lifestyle as Purposeful Life*
   - Consider brands moving beyond selling an aspirational or fantasy lifestyle dream to presenting a positive and purposeful life.
   - The fanciful lifestyle that brands project is often unachievable and unsustainable, driving negative consumerism and self-image.
   - A brand's effect on the consumer should be reimagined beyond the aspirational and towards the purposeful.
6. *Reimagine Outreach as Outlook*
   - Move brands beyond the relentless outreach to consumers, which is driving what seems like perpetual content churn and unconscious consumption, and replace this with a projection of a positive outlook.
   - This means no longer mindlessly feeding the content beast but repurposing communication to be a declaration of belief in positive impacts.
   - A more principled and considered brand articulation will change perception and consumer behaviour.
7. *Reimagine Digital as Physical*
   - Brands can use the digital sphere to connect their digital outlook and experiences.
   - For the first time in human history, the world's population is pervasively connected via smartphone, which can enable reaching more people than a physical reality and a physical experience ever could.
   - This abdicates location from brand to consumer, and digital communities can create infinitely customised brand rituals and moments.

6.5 REGENERATIVE PRODUCT PROTOCOLS

1. *Reimagine the Product as the Byproduct*
   - Brands can start to see their product as the byproduct, to reduce impact on the planet.
   - As they evolve beyond a fixation on product creation and transaction, they can seek new and innovative ways to monetise their offering.
   - Brands must commoditise experiences and memories to build communities, defined by what they do rather than what they own.
2. *Reimagine Fixed as Circular*
   - Knowledge fixed in brand and product can be redesigned to flow with circularity across nested systems, to be regenerative.
   - The process of making a product and using a product should no longer be linear.
   - Circularity is thinking about the lifespan of a physical product in 360 degrees rather than 180 degrees while capturing and productising the latent knowledge, experience and intelligence generated along the way.
3. *Reimagine Regenerative Sourcing*
   - Regenerative sourcing can provide a wider positive ripple effect around the supplier base to deliver positive impact for those places and people.
   - This can help realise a positive impact on the community of source material suppliers, their staff and wider nested ecosystems.
   - Sourcing processes should be open and mutual, delivering the collective benefits of knowledge and intelligence.

4. *Reimagine Regenerative Manufacturing*
   - Regenerative manufacturing can also always provide a wider positive ripple around the manufacturing base.
   - It can help ensure a positive impact on the community of manufacturers, their staff, families and wider communities.
   - Manufacturing processes should be regenerative, to yield a positive impact on finite resources, aiming to contribute to global replenishment rather than depletion.
5. *Reimagine High Functional and Aesthetic Lifespan*
   - Products must justify their existence in terms of costs and implications of production for the planet.
   - This means they should be designed with a timeless philosophy, to last and have enduring value for the initial user and potential future users. If they last a long time, you must still want to wear them or use them; they must age gracefully.
   - This requires both a high functional and aesthetic lifespan, for enduring use and relevance.
6. *Reimagine Multi-Use Afterlife*
   - To be regenerative, products must have a primary purpose but different secondary purposes for a second life, extending their usable existence into the deep future.
   - When being designed, brands must be conscious of the second life that the products take on, past purchase and first-life use.
   - Brands must also think beyond sale transactions, to after-sale service and preserving enduring lifespan through replenishment, servicing and repair options.

7. *Reimagine Knowledge, Expertise and Experience*
   - Brands must start to see value in the deep knowledge, intelligence and experience that resides within them, which can have a wider positive impact beyond singular product creation, and beyond their initial consumer focus.
   - Knowledge is 'know-how' that has greater value across other skills and services.
   - Intelligence is the application and deployment of this knowledge into educational initiatives.
   - Experience is, then, the delivery of brand knowledge and intelligence to create consumer experiences that positively engage and build memories.

This chapter has charted a pathway through regenerative brand theory. In the following chapters, we will start to explore how theory becomes practice, in the pursuit of growth 'beyond zero.'

But before we get there, some moments of poignancy.

"BOB, IT'S NOT WHAT YOU'RE LOOKING AT THAT'S IMPORTANT. IT'S WHAT YOU SEE."

POIGNANT

MOMENTS

LONDON

When I arrived at the London College of Fashion (LCF) to start my degree in Product Design, I hadn't realised that Central Saint Martins even existed. Strangely, my school excluded us from applying to polytechnics or universities, and the fact that the LCF was listed as a college meant that it fell within the sphere of opportunities.

I came to realise that Central Saint Martins was the place with the greater reputation at the time. I explored the possibility of a transfer.

To my disappointment, they were either full or most probably just didn't want me.

It was, therefore, a moment of some personal poignancy when, years later, FreshBritain were able to forge an academic partnership with Central Saint Martins, to the point where they asked me to become a 'critical friend' of the university.

As Guinness says, 'Good things come to those who wait.'

MASSACHUSETTS

My family all come from Bradford, and on my father's side, they worked in the mills there. My great grandfather was a wool sorter. We have pictures of him in Massachusetts, where he would travel on business, sorting and selling wool.

When working at Converse, I was obliged to attend meetings in Boston once a month. I used to stay at the oldest hotel in town, which had this beautiful whiskey bar, and in order to fight jet lag, I'd stay awake as long as possible in the bar, drinking until I could no longer stay awake.

It was on these occasions that I used to think of my great grandfather selling wool in the general vicinity and consider the echo down the ages. I was there as a brand designer, but really, that's just another kind of salesman. So the salesman gene echoed through the ages, from Yorkshire to Boston.

This used to resonate with me as a lovely moment of cross-generational poignancy.

BOSTON

We were invited to be the first agency outside of Boston to work on the New Balance brand. We were commissioned to define the brand and articulate this in a Brand Bible. I arrived in town a couple of days early, to explore MIT and Harvard, and Boston as a running town, to really understand the meaning of place.

The critical mission was how to differentiate New Balance from Nike, and I couldn't get the 'tortoise and hare' metaphor out of my head — the hare being Nike and the tortoise New Balance. I also couldn't shake a quote I'd heard from Olympic gold-medal distance runner Emil Zátopek: *"To win something, run 100 metres. To experience something, run a marathon."*

I kind of had this sense that there was clear water emerging between the two brands, having to do with time and philosophy.

At the end of the trip, New Balance arranged for me to visit some stores with a New England area sales guy who had been in the business since it started. What they didn't tell me was that he had a significant facial disfigurement, which took me by surprise when I met him.

But when we visited the stores, I couldn't help but notice how much love and esteem this guy was held in by everyone who knew him. I also saw how this contrasted with the shock of strangers on the street who saw him for the first time.

As he dropped me at the airport, he asked what I thought was the critical difference between New Balance and Nike.

I explained what I thought about Zátopek's insight, and the hare and the tortoise, but in product terms, the one thing I couldn't put my finger on was how to deal with the fact that Nike shoes were beautiful and New Balance shoes were not.

He looked me directly in the eye and said, *"Bob, it's not what you're looking at that's important. It's what you see."*

A moment of brand poignancy if ever there was one.

This still moves me to tears as I write about it.

CSM

Photo Credit: Jim Yeomans

FRESHBRITAIN WERE ABLE TO FORGE AN ACADEMIC PARTNERSHIP WITH CENTRAL SAINT MARTINS, TO THE POINT WHERE THEY ASKED ME TO BECOME A
'CRITICAL FRIEND' OF THE UNIVERSITY.

7. GROWTH IN PERPETUITY (IN PRACTICE)

Now, through the regenerative thinking approach we've been talking about in theory, we'll take a look at putting this all into practice, with relevant case studies.

7.1 REIMAGINE BELIEFS AS STRATEGY — RAPHA

Rapha put beliefs at the heart of strategy.

Simon Mottram did not start the cycling and lifestyle company with the mission to generate enormous revenues. Instead, he had a belief that he could help make cycling the most loved sport in the world. But through that conviction and the organisational behaviours it created, he has built a £220 million brand.

I got to know Simon at the start of his Rapha story. While we never formally worked together, over many Soho lunches, we've shared ideas, strategies and advice. His unwavering belief that he could take cycling to great new heights manifested in many milestones along the way. While some were a direct consequence of his quest, others were indirectly influenced by his beliefs, as they were shared and acted upon by others.

The company's *Kings of Pain* book, a collection of images and stories exploring the icons professional cycling, is to my mind one of the most influential brand books ever written. And *Rouleur Magazine,* a Rapha collaboration with journalist and author Guy Andrews that evangelised cycling culture, pioneered the type of brand content that would become commonplace as we moved deeper into this century. To wit:

2011 BBC Sports Personality of the Year: Mark Cavendish. The moment Cycling emerged from a niche UK sport and into the mainstream. I wrote Simon at Rapha the day after: "You are on your way. This is massive."

2012 Olympic Games, London: Of the 29 Team Great Britain gold medals in total, cycling wins eight. The most successful, and now possibly the most loved, sport.

2013 Tour de France: Rapha-sponsored Team Sky shares in three Yellow Jersey successes.

Beliefs shape behaviour, behaviour shapes results.

7.2 REIMAGINE 'TOP-DOWN AS PEOPLE-UP' — GOOGLE

Google's stated purpose is to *"organise the world's information and make it universally accessible and useful."* They have been making this possible by working directly with successive generations so that the future of 'search' continues to help people find information quickly and easily.

The tech multinational has been at the forefront of the internet revolution as the 21st century's reining home of search, and it's continuing this leadership by co-creating with Gen Z to define the future of digital information search. In 2021, Google created an advisory group it dubbed the Gen Z Council.

Erin Muntzert, the company's Insights and Innovation Lead, positioned it this way: *"Youth are changing the way we search for information, consume information visually, and discover new content — focusing more on social platforms and less on traditional search engines. Our Gen Z Council was one of those ways; it's highly qualitative and it feels very different from the type of research we normally do. It was far less about getting to like a singular product solution and far more about using the ideas to more deeply connect and understand their needs and behaviours."*

The small council is a global cohort of young people aged 16–25 that advises Google's various research and product teams on user experience and content consumption. It also participates in live workshops with developers and research experts.

Google is shaping lives and inspiring younger generations by co-creating with those who are shaping the future, putting people at the centre.

In a way, Google has always been 'people-first,' in much the same way as Levi's was at its inception. The jeans brand's founder, San Francisco dry goods merchant Levi Strauss, realised that while there was money to be made prospecting in the 19th-century California gold rush, there was more to be earned by helping those searching for gold with sturdy provisions and equipment. This people-first strategy has been echoed by Google from its headquarters in Mountain View, a San Francisco Bay-area town that began as a gold rush stagecoach stop. It saw that there was profit in providing access to the internet, just as Levi's profited from providing access to the gold fields.

People-first has been a successful strategy for centuries.

7.3 REIMAGINE SINGULARITY
AS MUTUALITY — LUSH

Cosmetic products maker Lush invented the bath bomb, that fizzy orb of fragrant extracts for the tub, and markets it along with a variety of soaps, shampoos, scrubs and masks. Founded in 1995 in Poole, UK, the company embraces diverse ideas and people and takes an alternative approach to a workforce ecosystem.

It is not structured in a traditional way — the majority of employees don't have an official job title, and they take on lots of roles to collaboratively help the business flourish. People progress via the connections they make. As the company characterises it: *"The more people you work with, collaborate with, support and are supported by, the more integral you become."*

Lush describes its working style as *"flexible, fluid, supportive, and if you've got the drive to push yourself and try different things, you will have our support."*

The term they use to describe this mode of working is 'mycelium,' after the underground network thread-like roots of fungi, which act as a 'wood-wide web' for the forest — nature's internet, an interconnected hive of cooperation.

Mutuality within this business model extends to putting 10% of the company's shares into the Lush Employee Benefit Trust (EBT). The employees' stock is looked after on their behalf by five trustees.

Mutuality is not a common concept, but it's not a new one either. In 1863, the Co-op was founded on Toad Lane in Rochdale, a town in Greater Manchester. One and a half centuries later, it now comprises 2,500 stores nationwide. Based on nominative determinism, it does what its name suggests. The cooperation of workers creates a market, enabling them to mutually benefit from lower prices as they buy in bulk. Probably the original example of mutuality.

A client we are very proud to have worked with is Gore. We helped design their Gore Bikewear, Gore Runwear and Gore One brands. As it is at Lush, Gore employees do not tend to have job titles that define their position. They work in an ecosystem of mutuality and cooperation, to great effect. In 2023, the company reported sales of close to $5 billion.

Mutuality is not new, but it is proven and successful.

7.4 REIMAGINE METRICS
AS IMPACTS — PATAGONIA

Measuring institutional change and changing a business model from traditional growth metrics towards positive impact is exemplified by the trailblazer Patagonia.

In 2022, founder Yvon Chouinard and his family transferred ownership of the company to the newly created Patagonia Purpose Trust and the not-for-profit organisation The Holdfast Collective. These two entities ensure that all of Patagonia's profits go towards combating climate change and protecting underdeveloped land around the world.

"A company doesn't last 100 years by chasing endless growth," Chouinard said. "There's an ideal size for every business and, when companies outgrow that, they die. We know we must be intentional in our growth to be around for another 50 years, so we're focused on longevity, not expansion."

Patagonia has redesigned their metrics to be planet-centric, not profit-centric.

I've worked for almost every outdoor brand, with the exception of Patagonia. Over the years, I've met the company on the battlefield of commerce, when I've been designing for the likes of Salomon, Arc'teryx, Mountain Equipment, Nike and New Balance. And I can tell you, it is an absolute truth that in the redesign of the brands that were in competition with them, we were endlessly influenced by the impact and position of Patagonia.

That's proof positive that individual company metrics don't tell the whole story, impacts do.

7.5 REIMAGINE EXTERNAL AS INTERNAL — VICTORIA'S SECRET

Victoria's Secret, one of the most famous lingerie brands in the world, was humbled by the voices of women worldwide. Listening to the outcry, the brand acknowledged its contribution to promoting unrealistic and unhealthy beauty standards, including objectifying and sexualising women and excluding those of diverse sizes, shapes, colours and identities.

Understanding shifts in society, and in response to changing views on body image, the brand turned inward, sparking significant transformation by redefining not just itself but also the very idea of 'sexy.'

The company brought in new leadership, introduced innovative programmes like the VS Collective, which features a diverse group of women embodying the brand's new values and vision, and created the VS Global Fund for Women's Cancers. Additionally, it expanded product lines to cover more sizes and shapes and even launched a maternity line.

Its marketing was transformed by embracing diversity, featuring a wider range of models and curvy mannequins in stores. This is a clear example of external factors driving internal reflection, followed by an external response; in this case, a major repositioning.

As consumers of storytelling, there is nothing we like more than a redemption story. Brands are not immune to the power of redemption.

Uncle Ben's was for decades the best-selling rice in the US. Through the years, though, its marketing was criticised for perpetuating insensitive racial stereotypes.

Titles such as 'uncle' and 'aunt' were used in southern states to refer to Black people instead of the region's more formal and respectful honorifics, 'miss' or 'mister.' The product's name was supposedly inspired by a Texas farmer known for his high-quality rice, and the head waiter at a fancy Chicago restaurant, Frank Brown, posed as the face of the brand, which launched in 1947.

In 2020, owner Mars Inc. announced that Uncle Ben's had changed its name to Ben's Original, and the image of a smiling, elderly African-American man in a bow tie — which critics said was reminiscent of servitude — was being removed from its packaging. The rebranded product appeared in stores the following year. Within three months of the makeover, the brand's perception improved favourably, with 93% of earned reach being positive or neutral and market share increasing by 10%.

Brand redemption can be a powerful force for good, but it requires that we turn internal reflection into external action.

7.6 REIMAGINE WHAT IS
AS WHAT IF — OMEAT

What if we could eat beef without killing cows?

The cultivated meat brand Omeat is pioneering a scalable way to grow delicious, nourishing and affordable meat from cells, outside the animal. With just one cow providing plasma once a week, the Los Angeles-based company can humanely create many cows' worth of 100% real beef annually, without sacrificing a single animal.

This revolution is being led by Ali Khademhosseini, one of the top tissue biologists in the world. Ali trained at MIT under Moderna co-founder Bob Langer and taught at the Harvard–MIT's Health Sciences and Technology department.

We were approached by the investors in Omeat to help them design a brand that could successfully launch in a volatile marketplace with many vested interests — including the likes of the US Cattlemen's Association and powerful lawmakers from traditional ranching states — aggressively protecting their position.

We went into this with our eyes open and realised it was going to be an extraordinarily tough brand creation story. However, with the science behind the company and the very seductive question 'what if,' we decided to give it a go.

Omeat are very much in the early days of their journey, and I'm confident that they will be powered to success because the 'what if' question has fundamental moral truth — namely, what if there was a way to create scalable meat production without the killing of 1.5 billion cows globally every year?

Now there's a question worth exploring.

7.7 REIMAGINE HOMOGENEITY AS DIVERSITY — CHLOÉ

Riccardo Bellini, in his role as President and CEO of Paris-based luxury brand Chloé, evolved the brand into a B-Corp, certified as meeting high standards of social and environmental performance, accountability and transparency.

Bellini strategically appointed fashion designer Gabriela Hearst as the company's creative director, placing women at the forefront of Chloé's creative decisions. He also pioneered the development of a Social Performance & Leverage (SP&L) tool, aiming to elevate the brand's impact from mere legal compliance to positive contributions in people's lives along the supply chain.

The SP&L tool will help the brand evaluate suppliers' performance according to six key indicators: gender equality, living wage, diversity and inclusion, training, well-being and job quality.[19] This provides a holistic view of a product's social and environmental impact, enabling the organisation to measure, evaluate and visualise their positive impact on stakeholders, make changes and improvements to their practices and influence those of their suppliers.

FreshBritain used to work with the artist Louis Philo, brother of Phoebe Philo, Hearst's predecessor at Chloé. Phoebe's early career started in friendship and professional partnership with Stella McCartney. It's not hard to imagine that some of the ethics and meaning system that cemented that creative association have permeated into Chloé's DNA.

It's reasonable to think that the visionary efforts of brands like Stella McCartney and Chloé could turn a fashion industry based on planned obsolescence — and perpetuating the homogeneity of beautiful product on beautiful model in beautiful location, shot by celebrity photographer — into one that influences a more diverse future of positive, radical change.

A sobering counterpoint: At the time of writing, within 24 hours of being sworn in as the 47th President of the United States, Donald Trump signed an executive order ending all diversity, equity and inclusion programmes in the US Federal Government. A response issued by the governmental employees' union decried the move, saying such initiatives help build a government that "looks like the diverse population it serves."

7.8 REIMAGINE THE BRAND
AS THE EXPERIENCE — NIKE

Nike transcends the traditional product offering with meaningful experiences by becoming a platform for all athletes to connect.

"If you can run, you're an athlete," said Bill Bowerman, track and field coach and co-founder of Nike. Bowerman famously redefined

---

[19] Chloé's SP&L tool was born out of the company's Vision 2025 declaration to "measure, evaluate and visualise our positive social impact throughout our value chain." Gauging social impact means gaining better insight into the positive influence an organisation can have on stakeholders throughout their value chains, from raw material extraction to a product's end-of-life disposition. Chloé's methodology was developed in partnership with two schools, the Institut Français de la Mode (IFM) and the Conservatoire nationale des arts et métiers (CNAM), and reviewed by the consulting firm PricewaterhouseCoopers (PwC). The business management tool aims to integrate positive social impact into performance reports and accounting frameworks, weighed against environmental and financial performance criteria.
Source: http://www.chloe.com/us/chloe/wome/subhome/spl_section/

athletic footwear after becoming dissatisfied with running spikes that were heavy and bulky. In a quest to help runners slash seconds off their times, he became frustrated after writing to several footwear companies proposing ideas for improving shoes to better serve runners. After nobody accepted his suggestions, he took matters into his own hands.

With the guidance of a local cobbler, he learned how to make shoes. *"A shoe must be three things,"* he observed. *"It must be light, comfortable, and it's got to go the distance."* Bowerman's footwear innovations proved hugely influential, shaping Nike's ethos of leveraging athletes' insights to design transformative products.

Today, people can access the Nike customer loyalty programme via the company's website or through four different apps: The Nike App, Nike Run Club, Nike Training Club and SNKRS. The official Nike App is home to a rewards scheme, where members can access product information, view available rewards and peruse member-only collections. Anything done in the other three apps is then mirrored in the main Nike App. Programme members can also earn rewards by scanning the app in a Nike store or at events.

Within these platforms, Nike allows users to connect based on interest points, compete based on goals and create based on shared passions. As of early 2024, Nike had an estimated 160 million active loyalty members. App segmentation has seen significant growth, with revenue from the Nike App increasing by more than 50% in one year. Nike use data from their app to create new products, improve existing ones and optimise inventory. For example, when they saw that more users were doing yoga, they launched new yoga gear.

As we move into a new paradigm where consumers are more defined by what they do and less by what they own, Nike have the opportunity to redirect their persuasive communication and connect to a shared charisma with thoughtful brand experiences they can then monetise and grow, without unnecessarily adding to the world's supply of unneeded products. FreshBritain worked on the Nike ACG label and the Nike running programme, and I'm confident that the company will stand tall in the history of brand design as one of the first to successfully lead this charge.

7.9 REIMAGINE INTELLECTUAL PROPERTY AS PUBLIC PROPERTY — THE FIA

Brands have an incredible opportunity to leverage resources and IP for the greater good. Rather than hoarding assets, companies should consider how they can open source and share information more broadly to address the biggest shared challenges and have the greatest positive impact.

Imagine the influence the Fédération Internationale de l'Automobile (FIA) wields as the governing body of Formula One racing. By taking an active role in shaping the future of the automotive sector, it is uniquely positioned to drive transformative change.

Just as racing driver, lawyer and businessman Max Mosley championed global road safety initiatives during his presidency of the FIA, the next generation of leadership can become powerful regenerative influencers. When an organisation of that prominence decides to prioritise sustainability, environmental stewardship and social responsibility, the ripple effects will be felt throughout the auto industry.

By opening up their IP and lending their institutional weight to important causes, brands have the potential to catalyse widespread progress. It's not just about protecting our own interests but about leveraging our platforms and resources to create a better future for all. The possibilities are endless when brands choose to be forces for positive change.

During many conversations with David Richards, Chairman of the FIA Foundation, we discussed the profound impact that IP, if open sourced, can have as a force for good.

It was in those conversations that the notion of open sourcing FreshBritain's IP crystallised in my mind. I was struck by how this trove of designs, artistic works, trade secrets, strategies, tactics and brainpower — normally the preserve of clients who can afford six-figure sums — could be a force for good for brands that are just starting out. They need our knowledge to help them make the right choices, so their emergent brands can grow and become change agents.

Open sourcing IP as public property could be one of the biggest catalysers for change in 21st-century brand design.

7.10 REIMAGINE STORYTELLING AS STORY-DOING — ADIDAS

Adidas, as one of the top sports brands in the world, is using its global reach to change people's lives.

One of the company's missions is to increase female representation in its management positions (director level and above) globally, to more than 40% by 2025.

In 2021, the brand announced that it was partnering with the Black Women's Player Collective (BWPC) in the US to help change the game for underrepresented Black women and girls. Their partnership will help accelerate this historically underserved group's progress by breaking down barriers to minority youth access in football and creating opportunities for future generations.

Through this initiative, Adidas is working with the BWPC and the U.S. Soccer Foundation to install 12 mini-soccer pitches across Black communities. It is also working to reduce the school dropout rate for Black girls aged 8-15 in urban centres by creating soccer clinics in Atlanta, Durham, Orlando and Chicago.

Adidas will serve as a long-term partner in this effort to change the narrative of Black women and girls in football by demanding equity, representation and access at all levels of the game.

"We will always strive to expand the boundaries of human possibility, to include and unite people in sport, and to create a more sustainable world," the company stated.

During the COVID-19 crisis, we were asked by Adidas to help redesign their outdoor brand Terrex. Understanding that Adidas has a strong consumer franchise in the urban community, we also could see from data that these customers had a disproportionate lack of access to outdoor activities. The solution was to create a brand based on hyper-inclusivity. We were inspired by *The Gospel of Mary Magdalene* — an early Christian text that was suppressed for going against the patriarchal values of the Catholic Church — and her narrative of inclusivity for women.

The result was an all-embracing brand platform featuring stories and initiatives that encourage urban minorities to experience participative sports and the great outdoors.

All told, a great example of the power of story-doing over storytelling.

For the future of story-doing, look no further than Goodwall.

Goodwall co-founder Taha Bawa is an interesting character, who grew up with his brother skiing in Davos but also spending a lot of his time in the summer in refugee camps. His parents worked in senior posts at the UN and took the brothers to displaced persons camps, where they used to help hand out sweets. On the way home, the boys were always stuck by the difference between the downtrodden exiles and themselves. They concluded that it was largely down to opportunity and education.

They've subsequently devoted their lives to the creation of Goodwall, a social network dedicated to giving young people in the global south access to opportunity and education. The group exists to explore how brands can reach a billion global youth and move from storytelling towards story-doing. It exemplifies the notion of moving brands from communication initiatives towards impact initiatives.

Not storytelling, but pure, action-oriented story-doing. It aims to reframe brand purpose, developing initiatives and strategies so they can start to move brands towards stories delivering impact. One way of doing this is working with leaders in the world's biggest tech companies to explore how to combine education, enterprise and access.

7.11 REIMAGINE TIME SAVED AS TIME EXPERIENCED — APPLE

At Apple, people's experience throughout the entire customer life cycle is paramount, and the company prioritise this principle. The unique and informative store experience at Apple is cherished by people every time they visit.

For instance, Live at the Apple Store sessions treat visitors to events featuring various artists, musicians, photographers, speakers and filmmakers. The in-store experience extends to wellness activities and group sessions where customers can learn coding, enhance productivity skills and engage in art-making with their community.

The company go beyond just trying to attract customers, seeking to create valuable experiences for them.

"Appealing to your customers to come to you is essential," Apple have stated, *"but creating value for them is equally important as well."*

The concept of saving people time with an effective in-store experience is really powerful. It lets them enjoy more of their hard-earned time on things that are more meaningful in their lives, beyond a product experience. Full marks, Apple.

Nonetheless, the company still have work to do in addressing things like the planned obsolescence that's designed into their products. We will be watching this space with interest.

7.12 REIMAGINE LIFESTYLE AS PURPOSEFUL LIFE — DAYLESFORD ORGANIC

As we talked about earlier, Daylesford is a prime example of reimagining lifestyle as purposeful life, beyond the usual look and feel of a 'lifestyle' brand.

The organic farmshop's founder, Lady Carole Bamford, identified an opportunity to do better and built a brand based on a simple belief that food production could and should be better.

The moment Daylesford tips into profitability, it will be an Elon Musk moment, as when Tesla became profitable, moving from a dream into commercial reality.

Daylesford's £20 slow-grown, organic, free-range chicken may be expensive, but it's the £5 industrially-farmed chicken that costs the earth. Sustainable food production that gives back to nature comes at a price far less than that of the cheaper mass-produced product.

If it were to be open sourced, the knowledge developed through ethically raising poultry could help save the earth and feed a growing population.

Daylesford may be seen as a lifestyle brand, which, on the face of it, it is. However, there's a real purpose that underpins the company, whose stated aspiration is to *"live, eat and shop sustainably, ethically and in harmony with nature."*

And so, it is not just selling a lifestyle; it is a brand that exists to generate purposeful life.

7.13 REIMAGINE OUTREACH AS OUTLOOK — NATIONAL GEOGRAPHIC

National Geographic is the king of visual storytelling, helping people experience the world's people, places and animals in an authentic, unfiltered light.

With more than 279 million followers on Instagram, it is the platform's third-largest brand account, after the Instagram trade name itself and Nike. The organisation uses its voice on social media to raise awareness of issues like global warming, health, poverty and inequality. National Geographic's social platforms are highly educational and eye-opening, and it empowers contributing photographers to create a one-of-a-kind channel. Contributors write their own captions, sharing first-hand experiences and unique perspectives with users.

In a sense, the Washington-based not-for-profit has many of the characteristics of tribal behaviour. At the core of a tribe is the symbolisation of their outlook, and it cedes awareness and action to the fringes. Rather than pushing the continual-recruitment outreach strategies that many non-profits deploy, National Geographic use Instagram at their centre to convey the organisation's outlook and allow the public to adopt, share and contribute to the brand.

Adoption over recruitment has helped them attract more than 279 million followers on Instagram and 313 million annual views on TikTok.

7.14 REIMAGINE DIGITAL AS PHYSICAL — SWEATY BETTY

Sweaty Betty wanted to grow their audience in key regions while encouraging people to get active and enjoy the outdoors with the start of spring.

Through its 'Let's Go Outside' challenge, the women's active wear and lifestyle brand encouraged users of the digital community Strava to run, walk or hike 40 kilometres over two weeks to redeem a 'secret reward' (discount) and the chance to win £1,000 of Sweaty Betty gear. They partnered with Strava for this challenge with a shared belief that fitness is empowering.

Sweaty Betty promoted the programme across their organic and paid social channels, as well as through affiliate channels. The impact was impressive: there were 186,398 participants and 78% completed the challenge, with an average of 10 activities per participant.

The promotion was a good example of imagining physical and digital not as two separate things but as a single meaning articulated through two channels, which just happen to be physical and digital.

The beauty of digital is, of course, that brands can now operate outside the confines of physical geography. It doesn't matter where you're from — you can conceivably reach billions of smart phone users around the world.

It is a brave new digital world of opportunity.

7.15 REIMAGINE THE PRODUCT AS THE BYPRODUCT — TESLA

Tesla are known for their innovative electric vehicles, but the brand have taken it a step further by envisioning both the nuts and bolts product and the byproduct of sustainable energy.

The main product, the car, was reimagined in 2012 when Tesla began providing sustainable energy for their vehicles through their global network of high-speed Superchargers. This technology boasts an impressive 99.95% uptime, relies on 100% renewable energy and stands as the world's largest fast-charging network, with more than 60,000 plug and play Supercharger stations.

In 2016, Tesla's acquisition of SolarCity created the world's only integrated sustainable energy company, providing everything from power generation to storage to transportation.

Musk continues his free speech adventure on X, and as he ramps up financial support for politicians on both sides of the Atlantic—now playing a pivotal role in the new administration in Washington, and championing right wing players in the US, Britain, Germany and Canada—the future will determine whether he was on the right side of history or not.

Few can argue against the notion that he has changed the automotive industry for the better, and his search for sustainable life on and off Earth is strongly aligned with progress.

7.16 REIMAGINE FIXED AS CIRCULAR — THE NORTH FACE

To mark Earth Day in 2021, The North Face pledged to use recycled, regenerative or renewable sources for 100% of the primary fabrics used in their apparel by 2025. This effectively transitioned the beloved outdoor brand to a 'circular economy' model for their primary product components.

The company also announced three core initiatives:
- A free repair programme
- A clothing recycling programme, 'Clothes the Loop'
- A re-commerce platform, 'The North Face Renewed'

These measures help the company source better materials and enable their products to remain in use longer, in pursuit of circularity. The North Face released their first fully circular apparel line, the Alpine Polartec collection for men and women, in fall 2022.

Although these initiatives by the market leader are to be applauded, we must also recognise the impact and influence of smaller brands that help lead the way. One such brand, a FreshBritain favourite, is Swedish clothing company Houdini.

Founded in 1993, the 'Maximum Experience, Zero Impact' brand have been a driving force for circular product design in the outdoor apparel space, inspiring others in the sector to do the same.

7.17 REIMAGINE
REGENERATIVE SOURCING — VEJA

The French sneaker maker Veja is revolutionising material sourcing by increasing the economic value of forests in order to safeguard them. One of the main raw materials Veja acquires in bulk is Amazonian rubber. Between 2004 and 2022, the company purchased more than 2,600 tons of the stuff… purchased at five times the market price.

A kilogram of CVP (semi-processed rubber) goes for 2.50 Brazilian reals, and Veja paid a total of R$16,000 to rubber tappers in 2022. This price included a bonus for payments for social and environmental services (PSES), which address social welfare needs within a community and makes environmental protection efforts, focusing on the interconnectedness between human well-being and the natural environment.

The brand has been embraced by those who want to wear sneakers but purchase with a clear conscience. It remains to be seen whether these regenerative sourcing practices will be picked up by the world's other sneaker brands, but we have watched Veja's good works with great admiration and have seen how the business has gone from strength to strength.

7.18 REIMAGINE
REGENERATIVE MANUFACTURING — GUCCI

In Uruguay, Gucci launched the NATIVA Regenerative Agriculture Program in collaboration with Chargeurs Luxury Fibers, the world's largest wool-processing company. Through the initiative, Chargeurs will provide Gucci with 50 tons of regenerative wool a year.

NATIVA reinforces Gucci's commitment to responsibly sourced wool, which in 2022 accounted for 60% of the wool used in its apparel. The project involves 10 farms spanning 100,000 hectares of land and won the Climate Action Award at the 2024 CNMI Sustainable Fashion Awards.

The raw materials produced through these initiatives not only allow greater traceability, they bear the names and stories of their producers. This is one of the steps on the road to becoming more regenerative by design and making a real difference.

As luxury brands continue to struggle with the concept of regenerative sourcing and manufacturing, and consumer dissatisfaction with planned obsolescence grows, it is brands like Gucci and Chloé that are starting to lead the way in fashion and luxury.

Sectors that normally pride themselves on their opinion-leading position have now found themselves lagging behind consumer sensibilities and much further behind other, traditionally slower-to-change industries, such as automotive, which are leading in sustainable reinvention.

Opportunities abound for those in fashion and luxury to rise to the challenge, change their industry and inspire change in other industries. How wonderful if they were to boldly spearhead a regenerative future and prove that fashion can thrive without planned obsolescence.

7.19 REIMAGINE HIGH FUNCTIONAL & AESTHETIC LIFESPAN — VEILANCE

In 2009, Arc'teryx started a pioneering project that was to take the technologies and materials they'd innovated for the inhospitable environment of the mountain and deploy them in product designs for an urban setting.

This initiative, called Veilance, drew a hostile reaction from both outdoor enthusiasts and those inside the company who thought that a mountaineering-oriented brand should not be creating, as the tagline put it, 'Cold-weather solutions for the city's harshest days.'

I was involved in conversations around whether to continue or discontinue the project.

I firmly supported its continuation because I believed it held the potential for an amazingly powerful legacy — namely, that you could create a product with high functional life expectancy, and high aesthetic life expectancy and, in that way, represent the future of sustainable product design.

I'm glad to say that we won the argument, and Veilance lives on as a totem of long-lasting functional and design attributes. Veilance is quietly creating the space that other design and luxury brands could move towards as we navigate beyond planned obsolescence in apparel.

7.20 REIMAGINE MULTI-USE AFTERLIFE — MASSIMO DUTTI

The Spanish clothier Massimo Dutti want to help customers reuse and recycle. To this end, the company have set up containers to collect garments, footwear and accessories in some of their primary markets.

Through this collection programme, they are working with 45 non-profit organisations — companies that specialise in recycling and technology specialists to redirect used garments away from landfills.

The items collected are donated to non-profit entities, such as Caritas, The Red Cross, Oxfam and Cepf, which sort them for repair and resell them for social purposes, or recycling, including by waste management employees at risk of social exclusion.

In 2020, Massimo Dutti met its goal of reaching agreements of this kind with more than 40 entities around the world.

"The best way to mitigate waste generation," the company declared, *"is to reuse and recycle."*

It is combining two initiatives explored in my formative experiences with recycling. As detailed earlier, we'd recycle clothing that was no longer wanted by Oxfam and sell it as vintage at Camden market. And, at Converse, we invited people to recycle their old sneakers in favour of new ones and then carefully disposed of the old ones in as sustainable a way as possible at the time.

It comes back to the lesson I learned at New Balance: It's not what you are looking at, it's what you see that counts.

Where some see waste, a growing band of others sees value.

7.21 REIMAGINE KNOWLEDGE, EXPERTISE AND EXPERIENCE — ARC'TERYX

Arc'teryx believes in the power of the mountains. Connecting with the mountains is the organisation's reason for being, and their inspiration to always find a better way. Founded by climbers in 1989, Arc'teryx has been anchored in climbing since inception, and with 36 years of experience it recognises the potential of its knowledge to go further, to have a positive impact.

"Our origins in climbing are at the heart of what the brand is about," said Jurgen Watts, the company's Senior Director of Brand Experience. "We are committed to supporting ways for new and elite climbers to experience the sport." It's doing so through programmes like these:

- *Arc'teryx Academy* — This is a collection of events for learning, connecting and deepening people's experience with the outdoors. Participants are given a safe and supportive space to advance their technical skills, gain confidence and learn from the best in the field. Four days, 20 international Arc'teryx athletes, 1,000 people per annum and endless expertise gained.
- *Arc'teryx NextGen Climb Commitment* — The brand are promoting diverse and equitable access to climbing. In 2022, they invested $5 million in community leaders and organisations who are advancing this access and those who support the highest level of the sport. This is investment through tactical support, such as passes to gyms, free safety-rope tests and handling certification, and free or price-reduced mountaineering courses.

- *Together Among Mountains* — The brand give to community-based grassroots organisations that help bring people into the outdoors safely, equitably and sustainably. In 2024, it split 75,000 Canadian dollars — 100% of the proceeds from its No Wasted Days film — between nine organisations, helping improve access to natural spaces for Black, Indigenous and People of Colour communities, as well as LGBTQIA2S+ individuals, bringing unprecedented diversity into the outdoors.

7.22 WESTINGTON, NUIE DESIGN CO & MAD ABOUT LAND

The power of the natural environment to unlock human potential has also shaped our work at Westington.

Still in its infancy, this initiative aims to optimise global human potential, exploring digital and physical as one and delivering access to education and enterprise platforms.

Guided by Suzy and Tom Smith of WHSmith booksellers heritage, the group are redeveloping an old quarry in the Cotswolds to become the home of a regenerative incubator. The idea is to create a knowledge pathway from university through to a postgraduate MBA so that a student's idea can be augmented with a business plan, paired with an incubator for the relevant commercial expertise and nurtured into a reality. The vision is to give flight to a new generation of regenerative brands.

Nuie Design Co and FreshBritain are developing a partnership with Central Saint Martins to continuously explore the 21 protocols in this chapter, so that Nuie's products can be developed onto a regenerative pathway. The knowledge and intelligence captured for this open and fluid initiative will create a route for talent from CSM to gain much-needed experience for Nuie. An important aspect will be open sourcing, provisioning the knowledge for the greater regenerative good.

Madresfield is an agricultural estate in Malvern, Worcestershire. The founders have a simple aim: to leave the land better than they found it. This philosophy has been manifested in Mad About Land, a newly created gardening brand.

Mad About Land have agreed to be a 'regenerative canary.' Madresfield have agreed to test in practice whatever is discovered in theory during the exploration of the Nuie-CSM initiative's 21 protocols. The challenges and opportunities will be open sourced to the rest of the world, spotlighting best practices and helping companies understand the pros and cons of actions that could be deployed within their own brands.

This chapter has explored regenerative practices from many companies. Individually, they are not the whole solution for sustainable life on earth, but collectively, they will ladder up to significant positive impact. They may not provide the silver bullet, but they'll help extend the window of opportunity for someone in our future, perhaps not yet born, to discover it.

In that future, it will be worth looking out for moments of serendipity to guide the way.

> "THE CLIENT LOVED THE MOON THAT WE HIT, UNAWARE THAT WE HAD NOT HIT THE STARS WE WERE AIMING FOR."

MOMENTS OF SERENDIPITY

SKY

When we were working for a corporate finance company from Manchester, they came to London for a workshop on redesigning their brand. I took them to one of the private-member clubs, where the clients bumped into somebody they'd recently met on a ski trip. Pleasantries were exchanged, and we were introduced to one another: She was a Creative Director at Sky, and me, Creative Director of FreshBritain.

Fast forward a couple of months, and I was invited to attend the Legends of Football awards dinner. Unexpectedly, seated next to me was the Creative Director from Sky.

Going forward, we shared contacts, and our ecosystems have overlapped.

The fruits of that serendipity are yet to be revealed, but the one thing we're both certain of is that such fortuitous coincidences should never be ignored.

In time, all will be revealed.

STIHL

Working on a brand project for the gardening tools company STIHL, everything seemed to be going wrong for my project leader. He was struggling to see the wood from the trees. I invited him to my house for lunch, where I explained that it didn't matter what we were trying to achieve; what we would actually achieve would be good enough. No one is aware of the stars we're trying to reach; they only know the moon that we hit.

I explained to him that years before, this had happened to me on a photo shoot. Everything was going sideways, and I thought we were doomed, but the client ended up being incredibly generous and loved the moon that we hit, unaware that we had not hit the stars we were aiming for.

The project leader left feeling more comfortable, and I went back to my office. Incredibly, I had a voicemail waiting for me from the client I'd just been talking about. We hadn't spoken for more than a decade. Meeting again in his office some weeks later, he had a brochure for STIHL on his desk. I asked him whether he was doing any work with them, and he explained that he couldn't get a meeting with them. I said I thought I could arrange a call with them. What he didn't know was that years before, I'd been in a leadership therapy session, crying my eyes out, and the person comforting me was none other than CFO of STIHL.

Two very serendipitous moments... and we got the call.

REAL MADRID

The former President of Levi's, James Curleigh, called me to suggest that I meet his twin brother, John Curleigh, who was doing a project for Real Madrid football club.

Would I like to work with them? *"Of course,"* I replied. *"Ask him to meet me for dinner at the Groucho."*

When we met, I explained that there some weird connections between his family and mine. For one, my best friend's brother worked in the music business in London, and John's sister-in-law used to be his personal assistant.

John said that was amazing, and that his best friend was also in town and suggested that he join us for a drink. I said that would be nice, and he joined us an hour later. He explained that he was from Toronto but lived in Chicago because that was where his wife worked. I asked what she did, and he explained that she was the Head of Neuroscience at Northwestern University. I told him, *"I have a picture of your wife on my phone."*

A year before, I'd gone to see my best friend — the same one whose brother worked with John's sister-in-law — as he was being invested as one of the youngest professors in North America for his work in neuroscience. The woman handing out the investiture to my best friend was John Curleigh's best friend's wife.

Another crazy moment of serendipity... and we got the Real Madrid job.

THE BRAND NEW FUTURE

MAD ABOUT LAND

Photo Credit: Tim Gautrey

THE PHILOSOPHY OF THE FOUNDERS—TO LEAVE THE LAND BETTER THAN THEY FOUND IT—HAS BEEN MANIFESTED IN MAD ABOUT LAND.

THE BRAND NEW FUTURE

MAD ABOUT LAND

Photo Credit: Tim Gautrey

GROWTH IN PERPETUITY (IN PRACTICE)

8. HOPE

8.1 BLACK SWANS

A black swan event is a rare, unexpected occurrence that can have a global impact beyond the realm of normal expectations.

The spectre of black swan events — such as another global pandemic, extreme weather events, terrorist attacks, financial collapse — casts a long shadow over the socio-economic landscape. The future holds daunting challenges that could significantly impact brands' pursuit of perpetual growth.

General Sir Roland Walker, head of the British Army, said last year that the world had become so volatile that the country had three years — *"just enough time"* — to prepare for war. He told me rather ominously during a car ride together recently, *"I said that four months ago, there are black swans, and there are grey rhinos. The latter you can seeing coming, but you can't get out of the way. The former you don't see at all. I'd say my comments on war and preparation for war, as a consequence of global instability, are more rhino than swan."*

These black swan events could lead to years of economic depression, prolonged periods of reflation, a lost decade of organic growth and back peddling from social and environmental commitments. The scale of future challenges may far exceed the credit crisis of 2008 or the COVID-19 pandemic, striking at the very core of national identity and personal freedoms and posing long-term difficulties for brands.

The impact would be multifaceted, with difficult questions arising around who will bear the burden of defence and healthcare costs. Suppressed borrowing, economic activity and income accompanied by rising unemployment, higher costs of living and government interventions would necessitate drastic measures from policymakers, including debt restructuring, wealth redistribution and money printing.

In the face of these formidable threats, brands must rise to the occasion. They must be prepared and positioned to become an engine of post-black swan recovery. The key to navigating these challenges lies in fostering unparalleled creativity and productivity. Brands that can deploy creativity to drive down debt, increase income and reignite growth would be the most successful in the aftermath of such catastrophic events.

Innovation and, most importantly, productivity will be drivers of success, which comes down to creativity.

Creativity will be the catalyst that propels brands beyond the constraints of the black swans and towards a sustainable future. By ensuring that their creativity exceeds their income, brands can position themselves to ultimately achieve the goal of income exceeding debt. And that can pave the way for transformative initiatives that can move the economy beyond current (and future) challenges.

8.2 PROSPERITY IN PERPETUITY — HOPE IN THE FUTURE

Some political commentators believe that the UK should continue on a path of conventional growth and not prioritise growth beyond zero.

Their thesis is that Britain runs at 1% of world carbon emissions, and until the developing economies of China and India stop pursuing aggressive carbon-emitting growth that accelerates climate change, we would self-impose a competitive disadvantage if we were to pursue net-zero emissions. I would argue that this entirely misses the point, goes against the values of doing the right thing and ignores historical precedent. Throughout history, the UK has led change, driven by innovation that has transformed society and the world economy. During the Industrial Revolution, it drove the transformational change from an agrarian economy to an industrial one. The country was able to export technologies around the world, such as railways and steam power, as the world looked to Britain to help navigate the future. This significant period of change drove urbanisation, labour movements, scientific advancement and agriculture improvements, greatly changing economies and how people lived. From the Industrial Revolution to the more recent developments, British innovators and innovations have driven the engine of global progress. From Ada Lovelace, the first computer programmer, and steam pioneers like James Watt and Thomas Newcomen, to the foundational work of Tim Berners-Lee on the world wide web, which paved the way for the information age. From Edward Jenner creating the first vaccine in the 1790s to Dorothy Hodgkin advancing X-ray crystallography to visualise biomolecules and Anne McLaren leading developmental biology to pave the way for in-vitro fertilisation.

But we cannot be complacent. The UK must build on its innovative foundations to create a robust and agile economy that works for everyone and is fit for future generations. The next decade will be an important chapter, featuring abundant change. And innovation does not just happen in physical products. Software, art, design and a range of other less tangible innovations are also central to the modern economy. Innovation is the lifeblood of business. It allows businesses to compete, creating new products and services for their customers, and provides huge value for society.

"Some people see innovation as change," said Apple's Tim Cook, "but we have never really seen it like that. It's making things better."

This is exactly where we are now — on the cusp of transforming our economies from high carbon to low carbon. We are on the edge of creating a planet where we can live sustainably with 8 billion people today and more than 12 billion by the end of the century. As when Musk took Tesla into its first quarter of profitability and the battery-operated dream became a reality. This changed the automotive industry through influence and impact. Just like Tesla, if the UK is able to transfer from a high-carbon to a low-carbon economy and deliver significant enhancements in economic growth, this will require the creation of a new kinds of IP: in food production, automobiles, information, science and agriculture. Developments that can be productised, commoditised and exported to the rest of the world, as others pursue their low-carbon growth models.

In addition to running at 1% of world carbon emissions, the UK is home to 1% of the world's population. But it's also home to 14% of the world's Nobel laureates, which speaks to our disproportionately high ability to create, innovate and invent our way to a global future beyond net zero.

Can Britain or any nation with an eye to geopolitical influence have an impact? Yes!

I'm reminded of a trip to Jordan. On a bright, early morning, we tipped over the mountaintops and into the Jordan Valley. The River Jordan swept from right to left, from the Sea of Galilee down to the Dead Sea beneath us. In one panorama to the right, we could see the Golan Heights and the Sea of Galilee, then just into focus was Nazareth. As we travelled to the left, within our field of vision, we could just make out Bethlehem. From there we could see the baptism site of Jesus by John the Baptist. Then, just in our peripheral vision, we could see Jerusalem to the far left. Virtually within our line of sight, we could see the topography from which the world's most influential story happened. This is, of course, the story of Christ and the impact of Christianity over more than 2,000 years. Believe in the divine Jesus or not, the resounding impact of the story is immutable.

The distance is about the same as from Liverpool to Manchester or Manchester to Leeds. As I write this, I'm reminded of the serendipitous late-night meeting with the Mayor of Liverpool and the Mayor of Manchester that I shared earlier. I wonder at just how impactful and incredible it would be to turn the economies of Manchester and Liverpool (and, therefore, the economy of the north of England) to beyond zero. To a place where the future IP of beyond zero — as was the case with graphene, a material first isolated at the University of Manchester that's stronger than steel or diamond — is created in a location that symbolises to the rest of the world just what the people there are capable of. Manchester have done it once; they can do it again! The precedent is there. Companies and enterprises march into the future showing just what can be done when public policy is aligned with local private enterprise and supported by national and regional governments.

The opportunity is to show how a smaller local economy can transform growth at scale and prove that we can design economic growth above the threshold for purposeful economic need but below the threshold for unsustainable ecological life. We can demonstrate how we can design companies that are world class and local. We can take on the world and perform at the highest level, going beyond zero and demonstrating just what the north is capable of.

8.3 THE NUIE DESIGN CO — EXACTLY WHAT THE NORTH IS CAPABLE OF

In 2025, Nuie are aiming to build a company that will pioneer beyond zero and effectively redesign an entire sector: the bathroom industry.

We're setting out to reimagine an analogue, disintegrated, fragmented, rational and anachronistic sector and transform it with the Nuie Design Co.

Through the acquisition of key brands, products, companies and marketplaces, we will design a horizontal brand architecture. We envision constituent brands of exquisitely beautiful and modern design, sensibly priced to deliver sustainable, convention-breaking new bathroom experiences.

The programme will be supported by vertical manufacturing in China and the UAE, with integrated design in the Halifax Design Centre in West Yorkshire.

World-class innovation will be centred in the London innovation hub, with R&D partner University of the Arts London (UAL), Central Saint Martins.

Thought leadership will be enhanced and growth turbocharged as each brand is designed using the approach we have explored in this book.

We will apply the guidelines we've set out and demonstrated through the case studies to produce a compelling and addictive brand design and drive profit. It will be brand design emotionalising the multiple and driving enterprise value through a group of companies supported by brand mastery, product mastery and channel mastery.

They will aim to deploy the 21 regenerative protocols to move to zero and beyond, to secure a beautifully designed and lovingly priced beachhead in a profitable and sustainable future for brands and commerce.

This will be achieved by:
- Strategic vertical integration — a business strategy that involves a company taking ownership of more than one step of its supply chain.
- A portfolio of Nuie Design Co brands.
- A range of Nuie Design Co marketplaces.
- A network of Nuie Design Co manufacturing centres.
- A strategic approach to turbocharged growth across turbo-demography or explosive population growth.
- Tactical horizontal integration — a growth strategy where a company acquires or merges with a competitor or related business that operates in the same industry, with the goal of expanding market share, gaining an edge over rivals and increasing profitability.
- Profit efficiency through a European gateway.
- Transversal product portfolios — a product strategy that involves combining activities from different areas to offer a comprehensive solution.
- Ambitious culture and architecture, signifying purpose and trajectory.
- Integrated innovation, symbolising aspiration and reputation.
- Thought leadership, driving an influential profile.

This could be the next chapter in the history of British creativity and commerce.

8.4 THE NUIE DESIGN CO — A NEW APPROACH TO DESIGN

Nuie Design Co represents a radical new approach to design, encompassing the design of a company, brand, product and marketplace; pathways to revenue, profit and growth; and a regenerative future beyond zero.

Designed the Nuie way, their beautifully designed living is lovingly priced.

The Nuie app will allow customers to customise and design their own bathrooms, while the Nuie marketplace keeps choice and revenue within Nuie, offering verified products, assured designs and authenticated brands.

Nuie brand design turns the intangible into the tangible, with compelling design that recruits and addictive design that emotionalises:

1. The financial profile, with value creation strategy.
2. The fundamental value proposition to customers.
3. The evidence-based future value creation initiatives.
4. The unique characteristics, assets and capabilities that hold strategic value.
5. The macroeconomic trends necessary to realise full value.

Through this holistic approach, Nuie will be positioned to win the battle without potentially firing a shot.

NUIE

Design Credit: FreshBritain

DESIGNED THE NUIE WAY, THEIR BEAUTIFULLY
DESIGNED LIVING IS LOVINGLY PRICED.

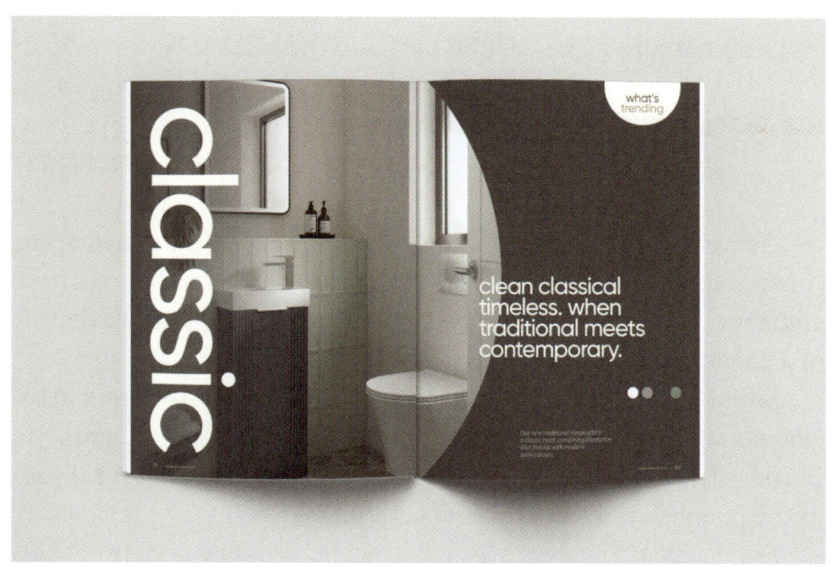

8.5 COMPELLING BRAND DESIGN DRIVING REVENUE GROWTH

Applying what we have shared, it is all about:
- Considering brand essence to define a compelling brand advantage.
- Leveraging product essence to define a compelling product advantage.
- Using brand world to define the sector and brand authority to define the compelling expertise and knowledge.
- Applying the lessons on the reason to believe to define compelling credibility and points of parity to define a sector's hygiene.
- Citing points of difference to define compelling positional advantage, with an addictive personality driving growth.
- Bringing this altogether, the brand personality can create an episodic and serial relation ship with the brand, which nourishes a personalised and emotional consumer relationship to drive growth and help win the battle.

8.6 ADDICTIVE BRAND DESIGN DRIVING PROFIT GROWTH

As we've laid out here, brands play a powerful role in shaping consumer addiction and loyalty. By defining a brand's place, ritual and time, companies can embed themselves deeply into the fabric of a consumer's life.

Brand place refers to the specific location or environment associated with a brand, fostering a sense of belonging and attachment. Brands strategically position themselves to become a natural part of the people's daily routine and activities.

Brand ritual involves the habitual behaviours and traditions that a brand becomes intertwined with. Brands can shape consumer addiction by creating and reinforcing specific rituals, such as morning coffee from a particular café or a weekly visit to a favourite store.

Brand time refers to the specific moments or temporal associations a brand cultivates. Brands may become linked to particular times of day, seasons or life events, becoming an integral part of a person's temporal landscape, such as Karrimor 'owning Monday mornings.'

Rational brand values appeal to the practical 'need' of consumers, highlighting the functional benefits and problem-solving capabilities of a product or service. These values shape addiction by convincing them that the brand is a necessary component of their life.

Emotional brand values, on the other hand, tap into consumers' 'wants' and desires, fostering a sense of aspiration, belonging or self-expression. These values create an emotional attachment that can lead to deeper brand addiction.

The *brand role* defines the personality and archetype the brand embodies, shaping one's relationship and attachment to the brand. People may become addicted to a brand's unique persona and the way it resonates with their own self-image or aspirations.

Brand effect refers to the emotional responses and cathartic experiences a brand can evoke, creating a sense of release, transformation or fulfilment for the consumer. This can lead to a powerful addiction as people seek to recapture these feelings through the brand.

What a brand *stands for*—its core values and beliefs—can shape consumer addiction through a sense of conviction and alignment with their own personal values and worldview. Conversely, what a brand *stands against* can also cultivate addiction through a sense of charisma and rebellion against societal norms or expectations.

Underpinning these brand-shaping strategies is the brand's *purpose*, which informs its vision, ambition and the broader impact it seeks to have on consumers and society. A strong, purposeful brand can foster a deep, lasting addiction that transcends mere functionality or emotional appeal.

8.7 EMOTIONALISED BRAND DESIGN
DRIVING ENTERPRISE VALUE

Nuie's vision is to transform outcomes across all its brands, driving growth through:
- Positioning aimed at turnover growth.
- Brand personality geared towards profit growth.
- Brand purpose driving corporate growth.

The brand's *mission* defines what is done every day to achieve the vision.

In this case, that revolves around moving beyond zero, towards regenerative sourcing, manufacturing, functionality and product design, as well as regenerative knowledge, intelligence, experience and brand design.

Nuie's higher *purpose* is to guide the brand towards creating tangible value on the balance sheet, showcasing the power of British creativity and commerce.

The most powerful value could be intangible — the example and influence the Nuie Design Co project has on other brands in other sectors that aim to emulate this journey towards sustainable growth, commerce and profit.

Nuie aspires to be a 'proof of concept' for The Brand New Future, demonstrating how a new brand can rise from nothing to become a multi-billion-pound regenerative entity within a decade.

In doing so, it will exemplify the potential for brands to drive positive change, transforming outcomes through a relentless focus on growth that moves beyond zero into a new era of regenerative design, intelligence and commercial success.

In the near future, we will be looking at other ways undergraduate, post-graduate and short-course brand design curricula can blaze a trail from creativity to investment, from education to enterprise, from the studio to the boardroom.

8.8 INFLUENCE AND IMPACT

As described in earlier chapters, over the past quarter-century, we've had the privilege of designing or redesigning more than 250 brands across a broad array of sectors: outdoor, sport, fashion, automotive, defence, commodities, places, private equity and food.

And while this has very much been driven by the profit motive and personal ambition, we've talked here about how there's now a more enlightened motivation driven by impact and influence. We have to consider the longer-term impacts of our efforts and successes and ask searching questions of ourselves.

We have asked difficult questions about balancing profit with sustainability and looked at how we lead by example. This has been shaped by deep self-reflection on:

- How we can help our clients move beyond zero.
- How we can encourage consumers to no longer be defined by what they own but what they do.
- How we lead by example and truly walk the talk.

We've detailed here our efforts to work through how we codify the knowledge, intelligence and experience gained in the designing of these hundreds of brands and open source it for communal gain. We've also discussed how can we do this in such a way that gives access to people who really need to make important and intelligent choices.

At any point in time, there are 100 million start-ups around the world that, during their fragile embryonic growth stages, need to make good and ethical brand-centric choices. These entrepreneurs are at the start of their brand creation journey, and many from the global south are among the 3.5 billion Asian middle-class citizens who are striving to live purposeful lives.

They want to start something; they are propelled by enterprise, but they do not have the budgets of those we've worked with. Nevertheless, they need to have the knowledge.

With this in mind, and in an effort to practise what we've been preaching, we have codified our knowledge and methodologies in partnership with Central Saint Martins. All of FreshBritain's IP — and the contents of this book — have been open sourced. (Go to: https://www.freshbritain.com/.) This means that for the first time, anyone anywhere in the world who needs assistance in making the right choices as they start their brands can access our knowledge, essentially free of charge.

My hope is that they will be able to create and grow brands with the knowledge and insight necessary to do that regeneratively and beyond zero from the get go. I am hoping that 250 brands turn into 25,000 brands, and then into 250,000 brands that are operating beyond zero around the world.

8.9 BRAND DESIGN IN EDUCATION

It's difficult to think about *the future of everything* and how we meet the challenges we've been talking about without thinking about the important role education plays in realising this ambition. As we have seen through the ages, education is the answer to moving people out of poverty and into a future that allows them to live and thrive.

Education is the answer to sharing the critical knowledge and answers to the key questions:
- What will be the value of intersectional subjects?
- How can lifelong learning enrich our educational lives?

- How can digital learning give greater access to the greatest educators?
- How can we eliminate waste to focus on doing 'good learning' rather than feel-bad experiences?
- Where can we connect commerce and creativity to promote value creation?
- How can we redesign educational metrics to include and value enterprise as much as employment?

The importance of intersectionality — overlapping or intersecting identities or related systems — is well demonstrated by Sony Music. The entertainment multinational had its first MP3 player headquartered in the technology division in Tokyo. Columbia Music, a label of Sony's, which had the most amazing rosters of artists, including Destiny's Child (featuring the young Beyoncé), were headquartered in the company's music division in New York. These two divisions rarely met, 'division' being an apt descriptor. They never intersected. It took Steve Jobs to realise that the intersection of technology and the liberal arts could be magic.

He took the tech platform of an MP3 player, intersected with talent through iTunes, and changed the entire music industry.

Education systems tend to work on a linear basis. The traditional model has singular subjects learned right up through higher education, with core subjects establishing conventional thinking and slow-build evolution.

It is at the outer edge of these subjects that unconventional thinking and revolution changes things. This is where innovating practices, philosophies and technologies grow wings. The magic starts to emerge at the borders of two or three subjects when they intersect, when new knowledge, new thinking and new opportunities collide chaotically. That's when blue-sky innovation starts to emerge, as proved so resoundingly by Jobs.

It would be interesting if we could start to redesign our education system not along linear lines concentrated on the classics, the sciences and the arts but along matrixed lines, looking for dynamic threads that exist when you overlap these subjects, creating new knowledge pathways, new ideas and new opportunities for future learning and growth.

Our inspirational leaders advocate that lifelong learning is key and stress that learning does not stop after formal education. Like breathing, learning is essential to our condition and continued growth.

But what if learning didn't stop when formal education comes to an end? Imagine that society encouraged the opportunity for continuous learning throughout our lives. To not do this seems to be a missed opportunity as we leave traditional higher education for the work-a-day world.

The only option as things are currently organised seems to be bursts of intense learning activity, such as MBA programmes or short courses. There could be much richer and deeper seams of accrued knowledge, experience and intelligence. Embedding the opportunity for lifelong learning into our working lives as something entirely normal, rather than exceptional events that today would interrupt the work routine, would accelerate human intellectual evolution. Instead, because 'that's the way it's always been done,' we apply the handbrake in our mid-twenties.

So much of education remains rooted in a geographical space, in the conventional classroom of old. But now, digital technology enables anyone with access to a mobile phone to participate in a virtually limitless courses, lectures, seminars, workshops, training modules and other forms of instruction. This presents a flexible array of opportunities to widen the sphere of influence of great educators, and great content, and spread it into places never before reached. Providing access to the highest quality educators and material to everyone means that more people than ever can access first-class education from wherever they sit.

It is time we stop thinking of universities as closed rooms entombed in Gothic architecture and unleash them as content providers and educational gardens. Let's start to think of them not as binary institutions but fluid ecosystems.

If you want to be an exceptional cobbler, you need an exceptional cobbler to show you how.

If you want to be a first-rate financial analyst, you need a first-rate financial analyst to show you how.

In both cases, you don't necessarily need a GCSE in maths, French or physics.

It's helpful to know that these are options for you, but you don't need to explore them in a greater depth than knowing they are not for you.

What's helpful in this regard is a continual review and adjustment process that enables you to go as deep as you need to in a specific subject area to assess whether it's right for you. If it doesn't strike a chord, you can then opt out and focus your energy elsewhere, in an area you have a passion for. That abiding love for something then focuses the energy you are 'good at,' rather than wasting time on something you're 'bad at.' As mentioned earlier, I went to fashion college without the requisite maths O Level. Had I not done that, you wouldn't be reading this book.

As we have already explored, 20% to 40% of the value of a company can be attributed to the value of its brand. Yet it's rare for someone from the creative arc to punch through to the boardroom, let alone get to CEO level. The hallowed C Suite is normally populated from the commercial or financial spheres, not the creative departments.

It's time for the creative industries to produce an educational platform that connects creative choices and brand choices to commercial choices and corporate choices. In doing that, they could pave a pathway from the studio to the corner office.

The bean counters and administrators know how to manage a company, but they are less intuitively disposed to the creation of the ideas and opportunities that can truly transform a company.

8.10 COMMERCE
AND CREATIVITY

Let's take another look at graphine. A couple of decades ago, a group at the University of Manchester discovered what is thought to be the most innovative material fabricated in the last hundred years. Made of pure carbon atoms, it is the world's thinnest material — just one atom thick — and is known for its strength, flexibility and conductivity. As we noted, this incredible stuff is stronger than steel or diamond. Really, an incredible innovation.

George Osborne, the UK's then Chancellor of the Exchequer, announced in 2012 that the government and China would co-invest in the graphine's development. Today, the majority of the patents for the material's applications are helped by China. And so it became the latest example of a global investment opportunity made possible by British creativity but not entirely capitalised on by the British.

It's clearly time to break the dead-end cycle. It's time as a nation for us to tie our investment community more deeply into our educational community. It's time that the inventiveness and creativity generated by a country that's home to 14% of the world's Nobel laureates is connected to a source of investment and commitment that brings a return back to our economy.

8.11 EMPLOYMENT
AND ENTERPRISE

As mentioned, today, the government measures the success of a university based on the number of students who gain employment upon completing a degree. Sadly, this only captures half the story, and half the aspirations of our student community, many of whom would love to be employed as they leave university but who have stepped into that long tradition of entrepreneurship. This means that those who want to start something, who want to make something, who want to create something, are not measured as part of the success of the university. As such, they're not invested in, measured or valued as they should be. The government must rethink its yardstick for success. It has to place greater value on personal enterprise and support programmes and policies that value and promote creative services in our education system and economy.

Having said that, it becomes clear that intersectional subjects, lifelong learning, digital access, more focus on prowess, connecting commerce and creativity and valuing personal enterprise should all play a role in the future of education.

To that end, we're involved in an effort with Central Saint Martins to design a course where senior executives from big companies will learn the principles of conventional brand design. They'll be given a primer on creation and positioning that generates turnover, personality, purpose, value and profit. And, importantly, the course will explore ways of turning their companies into beyond zero operations. Those executives will be sent back to their companies as beyond zero sleeper cells, who will transform those businesses from within.

Another initiative we're engaged in with Central Saint Martins will explore the creation of an undergraduate programme and a post-graduate track designed to capture the enterprise and energy that exists within Gen Z. The aim is to provide them with the qualifications, experience and knowledge to create their own brands, build their own companies beyond zero and, ultimately, gain access to incubation funding to turn their dreams into reality.

In the future, we will explore at new ways undergraduate, post-grad and short-course brand design curricula can pioneer new pathways from creativity to investment, from education to enterprise, from the studio to the boardroom.

A final initiative is to develop programmes with Goodwall that will enable brands to move beyond conventional ways of creating meaning and awareness. Typically, brands create an idea and then turn it into a piece of brand communication. This requires a stage-crafted process of casting, shooting, creating and production to manufacture a fake lifestyle or synthetic concept. That conceit is then pumped out through digital social content, advertising, print media and broadcast outlets, generating the meaning and awareness of a brand and connecting it to consumers.

We want to change this, which is why we're working with Goodwall to try and flip the model from synthetic storytelling to authentic story-doing. This is where the creation of meaning and awareness can be delivered through 'impact initiatives' that help connect consumers to experiences, to memories, to opportunities, to education and, ultimately, to initiatives that have a profound impact on those that need them.

We will be able to create initiatives that drive the meaning of a brand but with wider regenerative impact, delivering the same commercial gain as conventional advertising. Simply replacing storytelling with story-doing will augment commercial gain with the power of communal gain.

Through all this, we are hopefully walking the talk — through the educational initiatives with Central Saint Martins, the open-source opportunity, the development of story-doing initiatives with Goodwall, the proof-of-concept creation with Mad About Land and the power of example in the Nuie Design Co.

Our genuine objective is that over the next 25 years, we can take the platform of 250 redesigned brands and affect the trajectories of more than 250,000 new enterprises that will emerge in the global economy of tomorrow. Our genuine hope is that through the open sourcing of our knowledge, we can put those start-ups on a trajectory that takes the global economy beyond zero and has a much wider impact, influence and long-term sustainability than conventional brand thinking, with its closed, inward-facing profit motivation.

8.12 GEOGRAPHICALLY, WHERE IS GROWTH TO BE FOUND IN THE NEAR FUTURE?

The answer is Asia! The future growth opportunities lie unmistakably in Asia.

The key to global business success in the 21st century lies in this dynamic region, which is poised to become the epicentre of global consumer spending. As we've noted, by 2040, the region is projected to command 60% of the world's disposable income. This economic shift positions Asia as the natural home for both brand development and global market connectivity.

Success in the Asian market will be driven by a powerful combination of investment and operating expertise. This formula demands mastery across three critical domains: market understanding through localised investment partnerships, brand development led by global industry veterans and digital excellence supported by experienced operational and advisory teams.

The path to capturing this opportunity involves a multifaceted approach: investing in exceptional businesses and entrepreneurs, supporting emerging Asian brands and maintaining flexibility across various transaction types. Particular focus should be placed on the most dynamic and rapidly growing economies, specifically the Middle East-North Africa (GCC/MENA) region, Southeast Asia and India, where the next generation of entrepreneurs is emerging.

However, navigating the Asian market requires careful consideration of its complexity and diversity. As described earlier, the region encompasses 48 countries, 11 major religions and more than

2,000 languages, presenting both challenges and opportunities. Success depends on building robust relationship networks and developing deep consumer expertise to bridge these cultural and operational gaps.

The ultimate goal is twofold: building iconic global brands while facilitating bilateral opportunities — connecting Asia to the world and the world to Asia. This approach not only helps international firms navigate Asian complexity but also simplifies global expansion for Asian brands, creating a truly interconnected business ecosystem.

One person who's working to unlock Asian prosperity through this blueprint is a long-time client and friend of FreshBritain, Ravi Thakran, former Chairman of LVMH Asia and more recently managing partner in the private equity fund L Catterton Asia. With his new Asia growth fund, Turmeric Capital, Ravi and his investment strategy could be the key to unlocking zero and beyond in the region.

Along the way, we all need a helping hand.

"IT WAS DURING THE COURSE OF THE EIGHTH PINT THAT HE ASKED, WHAT IS IT THAT YOU DO?"

HELPING HAND

MOMENTS

HANSON

After not seeing each other for a year or so, my best friend from school and I went for a pint in Halifax. It was during the course of the eighth pint that he asked, *"What is it that you do?"*

I told him I kind of figure out the meaning of brands, help organise them, and then articulate them. And that helps transform the choices they can make and, ultimately, the performance they can achieve.

Leaning back in his chair, he said, *"You need to meet Tony."* A text message or two later and we were in a pub called The Hog's Head in Sowerby Bridge. I stood in front of Tony, now nursing my ninth pint.

Tony was a successful local entrepreneur with a bathroom business, which had a collection of owned brands that he needed some assistance with.

Given my state at the time, I figured the best way forward was enigma and mystery. I didn't say anything and allowed my friend to do the talking.

Nearly 10 years later, and we are working with Tony on what will become one of the most interesting projects in our company history as we build new brands to exist beyond zero in a regenerative and profitable future.

A helping hand from a very old and lovely friend.

CHIPS

Chips and I bonded over Bear Grylls stories during a meal in the Alps. We talked about Bear Grylls the iconic adventurer, Bear Grylls his classmate at Eton and Bear Grylls with whom I'd worked on his next-stage brand identity as The Guide Archetype.

Some years later, I was kindly invited to Chips' stag week hunting, shooting and fishing in the Scottish Highlands. It was over the course of that weekend that I got to know Jonathan Chenevix-Trench, then Chairman of Morgan Stanley International, and we discussed my work with Daylesford.

Jonathan and his wife Lucy then commissioned me to work on his brands at Madresfield Court, followed by the brand creation project that became Mad About Land with the Royal Horticultural Society.

In time, Jonathan then introduced me to Tom and Susie Smith (The Smiths of WHSmith), who we then worked with on their brands at Coulin, Camden and Westington.

Together, we are all working towards the development of the regenerative educational platforms and corporate brand and product protocols that should go on to help create a regenerative branded future.

Now there's the sort of helping hand that you don't often find on a stag night.

DAVID

David was the Managing Director of Converse Europe, and it was David who, over the course of a few years, promoted me from Marketing Assistant to Creative Director for Europe. He then introduced me to the growth equity firm 21 Invest, which hired me to the board of Karrimor as Creative Director. When we started FreshBritain, David commissioned the first work we did on Kangol, and in later years, he made introductions to the AMF corporation in France, where we worked on a number of their in-house brands.

Sadly, we lost David this year. He has been a helping hand who's sorely missed, as much for his friendship and energy as anything.

9. WHAT I HAVE LEARNED FROM OTHERS

9.1 CRAIG FORD — BILLIONAIRE BOYS CLUB

COOL

"Cool don't pay the bills."

It is relatively easy to make a brand cool, and it's relatively easy to make a brand into an instant commercial hit.

The hard part is keeping a brand credible and making it an enduring commercial success.

When a brand is the 'new' thing, it enjoys the spotlight of credibility in magazines, on social media and when talked about by influencers. From this position, delivering commercial success while retaining that magic is the artistry in brand design.

We've had the pleasure of working on many projects with Craig Ford, who has helped guide Bathing Ape, Stussy and now Billionaire Boys Club. We were able to achieve the difficult balance of credible and commercial with collaborative works together on Caterpillar, Dr. Martens and New Balance.

The trick is working hard to identify and deliver on opinion leading and early adopter third-party distribution. Delivering physical, tangible and tactile positioning.

Cool gets you a seat at the table, but it doesn't feed you. Hard graft feeds you.

Cool doesn't pay the bills, but it does help to get a brand going.

9.2 RACHEL THOMAS —
ARTIST

CHOICE

"Even 'no choice' has meaning."

While working with Rachel on the creation of the Salomon brand film, we were able to observe how she viewed every choice as creating meaning.

This was so with obvious conscious choices, in terms of editing style, music, footage and graphics, but also there in the less obvious, as with the silences and the pacing, at a deeper sub-conscious level. These showed how new meaning existed. The absences in silences created the powerful meaning of light and shade, throwing the action footage of mountain athletes doing amazing things into much sharper focus.

Thanks to Rachel, the meaning of choices has forever been imbedded as a core principle at FreshBritain.

9.3 JEREMY GUARD —
FOUNDER, ARC'TERYX

BALANCE

"Leave your ego at the door."

When I first met Jeremy, the first thing he said to me was, *"I hate people like you. All you do is sell adjectives."*

"You must love the Bible," I replied, *"because it only has the one adjective, which is holy."*

And, I added, *"We sometimes we throw in the odd verb and noun as an extra."*

With the mutual recognition that being bullied by his intellect was now off the table, we got off to a good start, and he revealed his amazing approach.

Jeremy would tell his designers to leave their ego at the door.

He considered any superfluous design flourish on a product not truthful to the design itself. He viewed unnecessary embellishment as an expression of a designer's rampant ego. He used to remove anything that caught his eye, much to the distress of his team.

He showed me the maximalist windows in the Palais de Justice in Paris. It was ostensibly the opposite of the minimalist Arc'teryx approach, but he said, *"Look! You don't see part of it, you see all of it."* If you look at an object and part of it catches your eye, that is what he would call design resistance.

"You never see a fucked-up mountain," he told me, *"and when you look at a truly beautiful woman, you don't see part of her, you see all of her."*

In other words, one thing should not stop you from seeing the whole thing.

This principle always reminded of Coco Chanel, who said, *"A truly elegant woman should always look in the mirror before leaving the house and then remove something."*

It is the essence of *less is more*.

9.4 ERIN SUMME-WHITEHEAD — FOUNDER, THANDEKA TRAVEL

INFLUENCE

"Someone needs you somewhere."

For a long time in my career, I was conscious that my contribution to the human condition had been limited to designing and selling great sneakers.

Then, I was invited to go on a trip to Rwanda with Erin. She introduced my kids and me to three enterprising young women who were starting companies with UN funding. During the course of the week, we were able to assist them by designing their logos, websites and content.

Hopefully, we helped give them a chance at success.

One of them, fair trade artisans' organisation Azizi Life, has developed into an amazing brand.

Erin revealed that our design skills can make a positive contribution to the human condition, over and above creating cool sneakers.

It was Erin who helped me see that brand design can influence positive change.

9.5 SIMON FOXTON —
FASHION EDITOR, *I-D* MAGAZINE

CHANGE

"Change happens when you choose to change."

As a student designer at Levi's, I was lucky enough to work with some influential contributors to street culture.

One of those was stylist Simon Foxton, who at the time was Fashion Editor at *i-D* magazine.

On occasion, I assisted Simon on his Levi's projects as a runner, working with other runners who went in to do great things. One of them, for example, went on to edit Vogue.

I was always struck by Simon's ability to venerate classic design and inspire modern fashion. He mixed and matched designs with a conviction that timeless icons seemed to share the same balance and lines, irrespective of where they sat in chronology. Simon would style things like a Dr. Martens 1460 with a vintage ball gown.

I remember being in a meeting with him about his next photo shoot for *i-D*. We had just completed a campaign around the rise of grunge in Seattle, all Courtney and Kurt-inspired dirty denim and All Stars. Simon announced that it was time for a change. *"Instead of drab denim, I'm going full-on colour and sportswear,"* he said. The ensuing shoot helped inspire the design language for the next decade.

Change for change's sake — sometimes a good thing.

9.6 STEPHEN MALE —
ART DIRECTOR, *I-D* MAGAZINE

SIMPLICITY

"No need to gild the lily."

At my first job at Converse, I was given £8,000 to create 500 brochures.

The job entailed orchestrating a photo shoot, designing the brochure and printing it. With that budget, it seemed economically impossible.

Once I roped in some friends to do the modelling, got a favour from an *i-D* magazine photographer, worked out how we could create four American-like locations in London — in a lake, on a rooftop, at a block of flats, in a basketball court, all within a few miles of each other — I figured we could get it all done in a day and then have a magazine print it as an insert.

It was a great success, but only because the people who we were creating it for had never heard of anything like it before. With no comparable reference point, they loved it.

Later, I met with Stephen Male, Art Director of *i-D*, and showed him my brochure. He gently showed me that it was in fact a design explosion. There was no architecture to the image-driver shots or the volume-bringer shots.

I had just thrown everything at it, and that's precisely what it looked like.

Stephen and I worked for the next three or four seasons on Converse, and then Caterpillar. For me, it was an apprenticeship.

He started to teach me, on each job, the need for balance, the need for space, the need for things to breathe, the importance of negative space to provide emphasis.

Then, also how to pace a narrative throughout a longer-form book or film.

These are all now critical elements in my toolbox.

9.7 ANDY TOWNE —
VICE PRESIDENT, AMER SPORTS

NETWORK

"Network your network."

Andy Towne first worked with us when he was leading Reebok.

The ultimate strategic 'monitor evaluator,' he'd been educated at Cambridge and risen through the ranks of fast-moving consumer goods. Andy is intensely analytical.

It was always with a little bit of dread that we used to go see him and subject ourselves to the depth of his dissection and analysis.

We went on to work together when Andy was responsible for both Salomon and Arc'teryx at the Amer group.

Both projects were a success, and in no small part down to his amazing ability to ask the right probing questions.

"Why should people believe?" "What needs to come true?" "What is true?"

The power of the insightful question is something I've always tried to nurture, but never have I seen it weaponised like an Andy Towne question.

Some years later, Andy came to see me and we were discussing our mutual futures. He asked, *"Do you know what true thing you're best at, Bob?"*

I thought for a moment. Was it strategy? Creative? Persuasion? Andy, said it was none of those.

"It's your network, and how you network your network."

That was revelatory. I didn't even realise that I had a network. To me, I just had clients.

From then on, I stopped seeing clients as clients and began to see them as an ecosystem of connections. Connections that, if brought together, could add value for each and every one of us, and build a really powerful ecosystem, and we'd be at its epicentre.

Sometimes, a fish can't see its own water!

9.8 TIM DELANEY —
FOUNDER, LEAGAS DELANEY

CONVICTION

"Nothing convinces like conviction."

Tim Delaney is one of the best copywriters of his generation — intelligent, intimidating, razor sharp, sharp tongued.

We never worked for Tim, but we worked *with* Tim.

We had a kind of partnership for a while. Us very much the junior and he the senior.

Tim has total confidence in his own ability and his own ideas.

He taught us that if you have an idea, you've got to commit to it and, moreover, you must present it with absolute and total conviction.

If you don't believe in it, why should anyone else?

9.9 SAM PITRODA —
INDIAN NATIONAL CONGRESS

THINK BIG

"World Redesign!"

The voice on the other end of the phone asked an amazing question.

"Bob, will you help me write my book?"

It was amazing because I was talking to Sam Pitroda, the father of digital India and the power behind the scenes of the Indian National Congress, Modi nemesis and stalwart friend to the Gandhi dynasty.

It was quite a privilege to be asked to help him write his book.

And then he told me the title of the book: *World Redesign.*

"Someone must think big," Sam said. *"Everybody tends to think small. Thinking big falls to you and me. If we don't think big, who will?"*

He stated that the world itself needed a redesign and asked if I was going to help.

I of course said yes. After all, how often do you get a chance to redesign the world?

The book, ultimately titled *Redesign the World: A Global Call to Action* and published in 2021, was a clarion call for a new socio-economic order based on sustainability, equality, equity, justice and inclusion.

It is true that people tend to aim within the sphere of what is possible. There are very few who aim towards and penetrate the sphere of what is impossible.

Someone has to think big. Why not you?

9.10 JAMES CURLEIGH — GLOBAL PRESIDENT, LEVI'S STRAUSS & CO.

WINNING

"Take the win."

We worked with James Curleigh at Levi's, Keen and Salomon.

It was at Salomon that he taught me how to recognise the win.

We spent three days in Chamonix with about 20 people, an assortment of category managers, country managers, product designers and brand specialists. We went round and round trying to agree on the future direction and vision for the Salomon brand.

After two days, we landed on a brilliant new positioning for the company. We had half a day to go. The project leader was keen to press into the afternoon and start to explore the brand's sports architecture.

James came over and said, *"Don't go there."*

"Instead," he told us, *"let's play tennis, go swimming, go out for a meal."*

Why not build on our success, with all the right people assembled, on a roll and feeling good?

"You've just got the biggest win in this company in the last 20 years. You have an agreement from all these disparate people on the future direction of the brand. You could unravel that good work with a misplaced conversation around product and sports architecture," James said. "Take the win!"

A very wise man, and possibly the world's best salesman.

He also gave us the best testimonial ever: *"FreshBritain Unfucks Brands."*

9.11 SIR DAVID BRAILSFORD — TEAM PRINCIPAL, TEAM SKY

TEAMSHIP

"Train like Germany, play like Brazil."

We were fortunate enough to work with Sir Dave Brailsford and Team Sky and see first-hand one of the world's best coaches deploy passion dispassionately as he designed a winning team.

The results that he managed to achieve at British Cycling and Team Sky changed the shape of British sport. In a very small way, we helped him see that imperfection and vulnerability could be a performance attribute when it comes to building love, affection and belonging within a team.

He is very much aware that he has transformed not only cycling but also the way we approach many sports. Those of us of a certain vintage can remember the disaster that was the Atlanta Olympic Games, with the UK winning just one medal. Since then, and since Sir Dave's tenure in cycling alone, we've taken more than 50 golds.

His approach to the team dynamic, the clarity and simplicity of the rules, everyone knowing what to do and when to do it, working intuitively and intelligently together, was transformative.

We adopted this in our own business — the notion of operating as a small, agile, adaptive unit — and it helped build our culture. It's how we can do really big projects, on multiple levels, for multiple clients, at the same time. We do it with precise, speedy decision-making and self-empowerment, delivering powerful creative solutions.

Sir Dave taught me that you have to earn your place at the top table.

This book is part of that journey.

9.12 LADY CAROLE BAMFORD — FOUNDER, DAYLESFORD ORGANIC

EXAMPLE

"The power of example."

Carole Gray Bamford, Baroness Bamford, OBE, could have just been really rich.

Instead, she saw the deficiencies and dangers in food production and the concerns this created for those around her and the wider society.

She set about redesigning the food production processes on her farm. Then, she set to building an iconic farm shop that became Daylesford Organic. Through the power of her example, she has influenced many others in similar enterprises and beyond.

Working with her and seeing the passion and love she brought to her craft, she seemed oblivious to her role as an organic trailblazer.

The massive lesson to us here is to realise that 'big' is not necessarily the solution to change.

Rather, real change can be catalysed and driven forward by setting an example. Influencing others to influence demonstrates how the power of example will eventually triumph over the example of power.

9.13 DAVID COCKCROFT —
FOUNDER, BLACKROSE

ADD VALUE

"The more lunches you have, the more people choose to work with you."

We first worked with David Cockroft at Sealskinz more than 15 years ago, and he and I became great friends.

We often discussed how best to comingle our networks to enable the free flow of projects.

It was David who said, *"Don't try monetising the network — the important thing is to network the network together in a way that adds value to people's lives."*

This takes a bit of a spiritual leap of faith.

There are some people who make a profession out of brokering introductions. We don't want to monetise those introductions.

We just want to make connections, introduce people to people, add value to those lives and know that somehow, having sent goodwill and a little commercial love into the universe, it will eventually make its way back, in some unknowable but positive karmic form. In a form that will benefit ourselves, the wider network, people peripheral to us, or all of the above.

The more lunches you have, the more love you create, the more people choose to work with you.

9.14 RAVI THAKRAN —
FOUNDER, TURMERIC CAPITAL

ASIA

"If you want to win in the 21st century, you have to win in Asia."

As mentioned earlier, I was once invited to speak at an LVMH meeting.

This was where my computer failed, my carefully crafted presentation went dark, and I improvised by asking a question rather than presenting the solution.

"What," I asked, *"is a brand?"*

From the audience of 30 young leaders, I got 30 different answers.

I left them with the observation that, as the up-and-coming captains of the world's biggest luxury brand, they should really have a unified understanding of what a brand is.

If they needed help with that, I said, they knew where to find me.

It was Ravi who came to find me.

"You've given me nightmares since that presentation," he told me.

It was during the next meeting that Ravi blew my mind with some simple statistics. By 2040, he said, 60% of the world's disposable income would be spent in Asia. That's an astounding $33 trillion.

To succeed in the 21st century, he told me, *"you have to win in Asia."*

We have to be able to address the addressable market, but as we have noted, that encompasses 48 countries, 11 major religions and over 2,000 languages. This is a profound input on our need, and hopefully our ability, to design not only brands but nations.

The big question, then, becomes how can we design brands — and build the structures and institutions — that can address the wants and needs that enable us to deliver and win in the global 21st century.

9.15 SANDY ALEXANDER —
FOUNDER, SANDY DUNLOP

EMOTION

"Few people buy a brand because it is like another brand."

It was while working on the Wrangler brand project that we were trying to explore the notion of emotional superiority.

There is no functional superiority in Wrangler jeans; they share the same characteristics as all other five-pocket western-style jeans. In terms of quality, they were on a par with the rest of their largely homogenous product category.

No one is going to buy Wrangler because it is a bit like Levi's or Lee. They will buy it because of emotional difference.

So, we were left trying to design emotional superiority into the brand. Emotional superiority creates emotional difference.

One of our colleagues on the project was specialist storyteller Sandy Alexander. He reasoned that storytelling has existed for 40,000 years, with a through line from Palaeolithic cave art to Greek mythology to Medieval minstrel songs to modern-day Hollywood. His logic (or magic) is that if you can tap into one of these stories, your brand will penetrate the consumer subconscious with a stronger and differentiated emotional connection.

For Wrangler, we explored outlaw stories in their various guises, from Robin Hood to Geronimo, and started to build a platform for our subconscious understanding of the outlaw narrative. Of lives ruled by rituals, not rules. Of being outside the establishment and fighting to change it.

At FreshBritain, we continued to work with Sandy on many more projects, eventually codifying his knowledge with our knowledge, and then with Central Saint Martins creating the brand meaning systems that many brands now work with.

Simply put, without Sandy's insight, knowledge, intelligence and help, we wouldn't be where we are today.

9.16 SOPHIE PHILLIPS —
CO-FOUNDER, FRESHBRITAIN

BELIEF

"When people start to ask for your opinion, you are on your way."

A source of self-belief is when others you respect and love show belief in you.

The cleverest, most intelligent, most beautiful woman in our college class went on to get a first in Fashion at the London College of Fashion, then a distinction in her MSc in Computer Science at UCL, before completing her PhD in Artificial Intelligence and Design.

When that person believes in you, it is an awesome source of self-belief.

We went in to build FreshBritain together.

When people you believe in then start to believe in what you say, that becomes the fuel for self-belief.

Once you become conscious and open to others' belief in you, it can become contagious.

In my career, I have been fortunate to have had the support of numerous amazing people.

They believed in me, but none more so at that start of my career when these fine individuals helped me by believing in me: Sophie Phillips, John Smith, Simon Rider, David Heys and Herve Bertrand.

When those you respect start to ask for your opinion, you know you are on your way.

When Herve asks you your opinion, you know you have arrived.

9.17 SOLDIER A —
SENIOR OFFICER, BRITISH SPECIAL FORCES

POSITIONING

"Winning the battle without firing a shot."

A senior officer in the British Special Forces taught me that the art of the elegant battle is to win the without firing a shot.

This calls for assuming a position so dominant that you can induce the enemy into surrendering because the odds are so undeniably stacked against them.

We translated this into positioning for Salomon, Volvo and Ben Sherman.

Bringing together clear positioning meant that we didn't have to drive meaning or awareness because other brands with fuzzy positions do that for you. Their positioning is rendered unclear in comparison to yours, which is crystal clear.

Brands don't have to develop big advertising campaigns when consumers can see who you are, see what you mean, see your difference and then gravitate towards your central meaning and understanding.

It was 'Soldier A' who helped us to see the potential of winning the battle without firing a shot.

9.18 NICLAS BORNLING —
BRAND DIRECTOR, SALOMON

COLLEGIATE

"Culture eats strategy for breakfast."

Niclas Bornling was the brand leader at Salomon.

The French sports clothing company had just been sold by Adidas so that Adidas could raise the capital to buy Reebok. Swept along in the shuffle, Salomon was suffering from a collective lack of confidence.

This was compounded by moving decades-old manufacturing offshore to China and the corporate grief over being let go by the mothership, Adidas.

Niclas asked FreshBritain to help them come up with a vision that would provide a North Star for their future. Instead of the conventional process — the agency listening, going away to brainstorm, and then coming back with three solutions for the brand select from — Niclas asked us to develop a collectivised approach.

He wanted us to solicit the entire organisation's input on what the brand could be and then set this in the context of the competitive landscape. After that, we were to work with the leadership team and come up with a shared vision of 'what if' for Salomon.

This was the first time we had ever pursued this sort of 360-degree approach. Today, it is the only way we run a brand vision project.

You can have a beautiful strategy, but unless everybody in the organisation believes in the vision, it's just going to sit in a drawer somewhere. If people can see their truth in the solution, they are more likely to get behind it and make it work.

This can be an important tool in the recalibration of company culture. As Amer Sports' Andy Towne told me, *"Culture eats strategy for breakfast."*

9.19 RODDY DARCY —
CREATIVE DIRECTOR, ARC'TERYX

EXPERIENCE

"Design loyalty beyond the point of sale."

Roddy Darcy was the head of innovation at Amer Sports and Arc'teryx, with a history of design and innovation at Patagonia and Haglöfs.

Roddy is one of the preeminent designers of his generation, somebody who lives and breathes mountain sports. It is his assertion that we should design the experience of the product beyond the point of sale.

Most designers are obsessed with getting the product to the cash register, with little effort given to the design of the experience of the product going forward, deep into the life of the consumer.

It is only in designing this experience that we're able to design loyalty, a lasting bond between the consumer and the product. Consequently, product design should be experience design, which is a brand design that will sustain profits and a consumer relationship long into the brand's future.

Designing the product experience beyond the point of sale should be part of the entire design process. Considering the human experience of the product is more likely to create 'product love' which will lead to 'product loyalty' and eventually onto the Holy Grail of 'brand loyalty' and then profitability.

9.20 TONY WOOD —
NUIE DESIGN CO

VISION

"What if?"

Having built Nuie from nothing into something, Tony is the living embodiment of turning 'what if' into 'what is.'

He is perpetually amazing, conjuring energy and experience with determination and sheer willpower.

9.21 MICHEAL SHEARD —
FATHER OF THE AUTHOR

SOMETHING

"Do something, and something happens."

As noted earlier, my dad used to say that you can't control whether the other people in the room are more talented than you, but you can control whether you work the hardest. This is a maxim for a strong work ethic.

He also used to say that if you do nothing, nothing happens. But if you do something, something will happen. *"So,"* he'd tell me, *"whatever you do, do something, and something happens."*

It sounds so simple, but if you believe in manifestation, by sending things out to the universe, they come back in ways you could never imagine. And if you keep doing something, the ripples you send out will keep coming back — you'll get tailwinds ahead of headwinds. There will be less resistance in your life and less risk because the planets will be continually aligning around your goals and strategies.

Just keep doing something, keep manifesting, keep thinking of what you want, and gradually, the universe designs ways of making it come true.

At some point you have turn to yourself to make it happen.

Thank you, dad. RIP.

"THE EVENT WAS BY NO MEANS A DEAD CERT, BUT WE HAD TO HAVE A GO, BECAUSE SOMEONE HAS TO."

MAKING IT HAPPEN

MOMENTS

CONVERSE

I was working as a Marketing Assistant at Converse, and getting nowhere, until my boss, who didn't want to make a presentation at a European sales conference, asked me to do it for him. It was supposed to detail how we were going to spend £50,000 to support the UK clothing brand he was working on.

I decided this was too good an opportunity to miss because it would put me in front of the Converse leadership team. But instead of explaining how I'd spend the £50,000, I presented a global marketing plan for the brand, articulating what they should be doing, which they weren't, which would help that £50,000 go a lot further.

This involved deploying strict distribution rules, bringing in product from Japan and reorienting the brand from basketball to athleisure.

The boss took me to one side afterwards and said, *"Son, that presentation gave me a hard-on."*

He promoted me within weeks.

Definitely a 'making it happen moment,' in every way.

LVMH

I got a call from one of LVMH's managing directors in Asia, saying he wanted to meet me in Milan. He had nine brands he wanted a point of view on and asked if I could meet him at 7am in the Armani café near La Scala for 20 minutes.

I had a week to prepare, and realising the café would be busy, I thought the best approach would be to produce nine one-minute films, one for each brand.

It meant turning the agency on its head for a week so I could simply press play and say, *"Here's what I think."*

I was also on a family ski holiday in Switzerland that week, so I'd have to get a taxi from Verbier to Milan at 3am, and travel three hours each way, with the round-trip costing £3,000.

To me it was worth it because I would have a private audience with a member of the LVMH leadership team, and I could show him what we were capable of by producing nine films within a week.

It worked. We immediately were asked to present this to the wider leadership team, which some months later resulted in a long-term contract with L Capital in Asia.

Another 'making it happen moment,' although the team were put under incredible strain. But they did an amazing job.

THE FUTURE OF EVERYTHING

As detailed earlier, The Future of Everything was an event we put on last year, and it became the source of inspiration for this book.

Prompted by our work to take a mountaineering brand to carbon neutrality and beyond, it has become the template for what we'd like to do to move all brands there in our effort to realise a regenerative future.

The event was by no means a dead cert, but we had to have a go, because someone has to.

The response below shows that sometimes 'making it happen moments' actually make it happen.

"Lovely" — UAL, Central Saint Martins
"Amazing" — Turmeric Capital
"Really Positive!"— Unicef
"Tour de force — dismayingly brilliant" — Mad About Land
"WOTADAY" — UAL, Central Saint Martins
"Thought-provoking" — Smythson
"Great to join FreshBritain" — Coca-Cola
"Brilliant disquieting, thought provoking, inspiring" — Westington

"The forefront of brand, fascinating and enlightening" — Bear Grylls
"A great event" — Madresfield
"Really enjoyed it" — Wildfarmed
"We were buzzing!" — Burberry
"All very inspiring!" — Volvo
"Fascinating, eye and mind opener" — Boggi Milano
"The room was buzzing" — The Foundation
"Brilliant" — Somerset House
"Brilliant morning" — Lotka & Co
"Intriguing" — F1A
"Insightful as ever" — New Era
"Incredibly thought provoking" — PieCrust
"It was excellent" — B2C
"Great job" — BoxFund

This book is another 'making it happen moment.'

10. CONCLUSION

It may be that by 2040, when population scientists project there will be 9 billion people living on Earth, humanity will have conspired to develop technologies and innovations that will enable that staggering crush of humanity to live sustainably on our planet.

History suggests this will be possible. We have risen to the challenge when our survival was threatened by diseases like the Spanish flu, the Black Death, Cholera and Smallpox. We conjured solutions that inspired a pathway through the deadly COVID-19 outbreak.

The difference with climate change and sustainable life on earth is that these issues won't be solved by the same sort of single-bullet solution. Instead, they demand an incredible array of technological advances, across all sectors of our economy. As we've outlined here, we'll need to achieve growth in a way that replenishes rather than depletes the planet.

This will come about through consumers choosing to buy brands that represent the future they want to see. That help sustain the world they want their grandchildren to live in. Nine billion consumer choices will be the democratic lever that creates the momentum for commerce to be redesigned, so these billions of people who will live on Earth will not be defined by what they own, but by what they do.

Will we have designed the innovations and created the advances required for sustainable life on earth within the next 15 years? We simply don't know.

If we can stabilise population growth in Africa and Asia, scientists suggest that by the end of the century, there will be 12 billion people living on our planet. This means that those who will create the innovations and the consumers who will consume these in a regenerative, positively impactful way by 2099 are likely not yet born.

The consumers of tomorrow will live in entirely different ways, with economies that will be created in entirely different ways. These are the innovators who will pioneer an entirely different way of living. They are the future.

As we discovered in earlier chapters, politicians are addicted to conventional economic growth because it enables them to make and deliver policy promises and retain their positions of power without increasing taxes. Conventional growth increases tax revenues without increasing tax rates and funds the policy promises. We cannot wait for politicians to create the space for the future to move into. We must do it. It falls to us as designers, creators, inventors, entrepreneurs, educators and consumers to lead the way.

Barack Obama said, *"We are the first generation to experience the impact of climate change and the last generation who can do something about it."*

We must be that generation.

We should recognise that we may not be 'Cathedral Builders.'

We might be among those who will find the solutions that benefit the generations yet to be born.

We might be the generation of 'Window Builders.'

We might be the ones who extend the window of time for coming generations to build the human race's tomorrow.

We can extend their window tomorrow by redesigning consumption and production today.

With every brand we buy, each one of us is a co-designer of future production and consumption.

We can buy the future we want to see.

We can buy sustainable life on earth.
The End. (Let's hope not!)

—

Dear Reader,
Well done, you got to the end.
Thank you for spending this time with me.
To wrap things up, just a few more moments of enlightenment.

"WE HAVE TO FIND WAYS TO GROW PROFITABLY WHILE DOING GOOD AND DOING RIGHT."

MOMENTS OF
ENLIGHTENMENT

OPPORTUNITY

Some years ago, we were working with Generation Investment Management, the private equity fund established by Al Gore, the environmental activist and former Vice President of the United States.

The sustainable investment group's basic argument was that we had a responsibility to move the planet to carbon neutral solutions because our future depended on it.

To some extent, they also relied on going into a room and telling people with non-carbon neutral investments that they were wrong.

You rarely win the room by declaring that everybody there is wrong. Rather, you'll stand more of a chance of success if you figure out a way of aligning your objective with theirs, so you can both be right.

The enlightened moment was when we realised the investment opportunity was being portrayed as a weighty responsibility, as the planet's 8 billion people move towards carbon-neutral solutions.

We changed the narrative so that responsibility became an opportunity, and it was positioned as an opportunity not in the future, but an investment opportunity right now.

Win the room by telling them they are right, and then sell them what they didn't know they needed.

INFLUENCE

It was while working for Daylesford Organic that I experienced a moment of enlightenment during a conversation with Lady Bamford.

I was explaining that I was reticent to work on the project unless a goal was to turn Daylesford into a profit-making enterprise.

My reasoning was that the farming operation was onto something in terms of transforming food production with organic and regenerative methodologies. Although Daylesford might never be the biggest in its space in terms of scale, it can become the most influential.

But being influential means people have to be able to copy you, and as a business, they're only likely to copy you if you make a profit.

This is a simple enough observation: you cannot overturn over 300 years of capitalism with good intentions alone.

We have to work with capitalism and consumerism to change the way we produce and create things.

We have to find ways to grow profitably while doing good and doing right, influencing more people to come over to this new way of thinking.

RELIGION

While I have never been particularly religious, I've always been interested in religions as branded meaning systems. I particularly love the metaphors in religious doctrine.

One thing all the world's religions share is the metaphor of the mountain.

In Judaism, through the teachings of Moses and Abraham, we rise up the mountain and reach meaningful life.

In Christianity, through the teachings of Jesus, we rise up the mountain and reach everlasting life.

In Islam, through the teachings of Mohammed, we rise up the mountain and reach paradise.

In Buddhism, through the teachings of the Buddha, we struggle up the mountain, and at the summit, we reach enlightenment.

In Hinduism, we also rise up the mountain, and at the summit, we realise quite a different thing. While all the other religions think that they are the only legitimate route to the summit, Hinduism tells us that it doesn't matter how you get up the mountain — the point is that we all get to the top.

Only Hinduism holds that all the other routes are equally legitimate ways to the top. Such a philosophy, with this simple observation, is the potential future for global religious tolerance.

This is why, when I worked for the Indian National Congress in India's general election, I realised that the ruling BJP party's brand of Hindu nationalism — that theirs would be the sole national-populist identity for the Indian subcontinent — was oxymoronic to the meaning of Hinduism itself.

This is how sometimes we can use our understanding of brands to help shape world events in unseen but extraordinary ways.